Hitler and Nazi Germany

CAMBRIDGE PERSPECTIVES IN HISTORY
Series editors: Richard Brown and David Smith

Other theme texts in the series include:

The Tudor monarchies, 1485–1603   John McGurk   0 521 59665 3

Authority and disorder in Tudor times, 1485–1603   Paul Thomas   0 521 62664 1

The Renaissance monarchies, 1469–1558   Catherine Mulgan   0 521 59870 2

Papists, Protestants and Puritans, 1559–1714   Diana Newton   0 521 59845 1

British imperialism, 1750–1970   Simon C. Smith   0 521 59930 X

Democracy and the state, 1830–1945   Michael Willis   0 521 59994 6

A disunited kingdom? 1800–1949   Christine Kinealy   0 521 59844 3

Chartism   Richard Brown   0 521 58617 8

Nationalism in Europe, 1789–1945   Timothy Baycroft   0 521 59871 0

Revolutions, 1789–1917   Allan Todd   0 521 58600 3

The origins of the First and Second World Wars   Frank McDonough   0 521 56861 7

Fascism   Richard Thurlow   0 521 59872 9

The Holocaust   Peter Neville   0 521 59501 0

Hitler and Nazi Germany

Frank McDonough

Senior Lecturer
Liverpool John Moores University

CAMBRIDGE
UNIVERSITY PRESS

For Ann – with love

PUBLISHED BY THE PRESS SYNDICATE OF THE UNIVERSITY OF CAMBRIDGE
The Pitt Building, Trumpington Street, Cambridge, United Kingdom

CAMBRIDGE UNIVERSITY PRESS
The Edinburgh Building, Cambridge CB2 2RU, UK
40 West 20th Street, New York, NY 10011–4211, USA
477 Williamstown Road, Port Melbourne, VIC 3207, Australia
Ruiz de Alarcón 13, 28014 Madrid, Spain
Dock House, The Waterfront, Cape Town 8001, South Africa

http://www.cambridge.org

First published 1999
Fifth printing 2003

Printed in the United Kingdom at the University Press, Cambridge

A catalogue record for this book is available from the British Library

ISBN 0 521 59502 9 paperback

Text design by Newton Harris Design Partnership

Map illustrations by Kathy Baxendale

2 ㅇㅇ 3 ㅇㅇ3 ㅇㅇㅇ

ACKNOWLEDGEMENTS
Cover, 49, 111, Peter Newark's Military Pictures; 12, Bildarchiv Preussischer
Kulturbesitz; 25, David King; 28, Mary Evans Picture Library; 38, 74, 108, 116,
134, Hulton Getty; 64, Bilderdienst Süddeutscher Verlag; 101, AKG London; 115,
Pearson Education.

The cover photograph shows Hitler at a party rally in the early 1930s.

The author would like to thank Bob Morley for his valuable advice on the
chapter on mass murder in Nazi Germany.

Contents

Contents

Introduction

No single historical figure dominates the history of the twentieth century in quite the same way as Adolf Hitler. It is very difficult to understand the incredible events which occurred in Nazi Germany from 1933 to 1945 without understanding the personality, the ideology and the career of this remarkable individual. The appearance of Hitler is instantly recognisable – the distinctive haircut, brushed into a side parting, the little moustache, the prominent nose, the square jaw and those intense, staring eyes. What we find difficult to understand is how such an ordinary-looking individual could have had such an extraordinary effect on world history.

This new study of Hitler and Nazi Germany, which is based on a wide range of sources, the most recent research and many previously unpublished documents, does not seek to downplay the importance of Hitler's unique and dynamic personality on the rise and fall of Nazi Germany, but at the same time it attempts to place Hitler's role and his motives within a broad-ranging social, economic and international framework. Each chapter in the book deals with a major aspect of the history of Nazi Germany and seeks to adopt a balance between opposing positions within the debate, where deemed appropriate, and to offer original assessments when deemed necessary. This approach allows for fresh insights on most of the major themes and issues related to the study of Hitler and Nazi Germany.

The book begins with an overview of the early life, ideology and rise to power of Adolf Hitler. In Chapter 2 there is a detailed analysis of the structure and nature of the Nazi state and economy. In Chapter 3, the focus shifts to the domestic aspects of the Nazi regime, including an examination of propaganda and indoctrination, and Nazi policies towards the family, women, education, youth, crime, health and culture. In Chapter 4, opposition and dissent within Nazi Germany are thoroughly investigated. Hitler's foreign policy in the years which led to the Second World War is fully explored in Chapter 5. In Chapter 6, the military strategy adopted by Hitler as war leader is systematically evaluated. Chapter 7 contains a detailed and thought-provoking reassessment of the origins and the implementation of the Holocaust. In Chapter 8, the concluding chapter, there is a broad-ranging assessment of the key problems in the vast historical debate surrounding the study of Hitler and Nazi Germany.

It is hoped this book will deepen the understanding of all those who wish to examine the key issues surrounding the study of this subject.

Adolf Hitler: early life, ideology and rise to power, 1889–1933

Family background and early life

Adolf Hitler's early life was fairly unremarkable. His family were not even German. They came originally from Waldviertel, a small village 50 miles north-west of Vienna, the Austrian capital. The supposed grandfather of the future Nazi dictator was Johann Georg Hiedler, a mill worker, who married Maria Anna Schicklgruber, a domestic servant, in May 1842. Their marriage came five years after Maria had given birth to a son, named Alois. On the birth register, the space where the name of the father should be is left blank. It is assumed Johann Georg Hiedler was the real father of Alois, but this has not been proven. Alois Hitler bore the name Schicklgruber until he was 40. He lived as a child with Johann Nepomuk Hiedler, his uncle. In 1877, Alois registered Johann Georg Hiedler as his father, but on the birth register Hiedler is spelt Hitler. This decision ensured that the future Nazi dictator was not called Adolf Schicklgruber. Thousands of Germans shouting 'Heil Schicklgruber' somehow does not sound right.

The private life of Alois Hitler was blighted by the death of his first two wives, a roving eye for the ladies, a nomadic nature and heavy drinking. He married Anna Glass in 1864, but she died (childless) in 1883. A month later, he wed Franziska Matzelberger, with whom he was already having an affair; indeed, the liaison had already produced a son: Alois Jnr. Just three months after this marriage, a daughter, Angela, was born. In 1884, his second wife died of tuberculosis. Needless to say, Alois had a third bride lined up. On 7 January 1885, Alois, by now 47, married Klara Poelzl, aged 24, his second cousin, the granddaughter of Johann Nepomuk Hiedler. Klara was pregnant on her wedding day and, given their close family relationship, the couple required a special dispensation from the Vatican to allow the marriage to go ahead.

Klara gave birth to six children during her marriage to Alois Hitler, four sons and two daughters, but apart from Adolf Hitler and his younger sister, Pauline, the remainder died in infancy. Adolf Hitler, the fourth child of the marriage, was born at 6.30 p.m. on 20 April 1889 in the Gasthof zum Pommer, an inn in the town of Braunau am Inn, Austria, close to the German border state of Bavaria. Adolf Hitler was baptised a Roman Catholic. On the birth register he is named Adolfus Hitler, but was always known as Adolf. Angela, his half-sister, was the only near relative he kept in close contact with in later life. Indeed, Angela's daughter, Geli Raubal, became the subject of Hitler's incestuous infatuation in the late 1920s, which no doubt contributed to her decision to commit suicide by shooting herself through the head in Hitler's Munich apartment in 1931.

Adolf Hitler seems to have genuinely loved his mother, who watched over him as a child, pampering him and letting him do what he liked. He always carried a picture of her in his wallet. In contrast, he was very hostile towards his father, who was strict and domineering. Alois demanded absolute obedience, often punishing bad behaviour by the use of a whip. Hitler described his relationship with his father as 'a battle of competing wills'. Alois wanted his son to become a senior civil servant, but young Adolf wanted to become an artist. Hitler later recalled: 'I never loved my father. I therefore feared him all the more. He had a terrible temper and often whipped me.'[1]

In *Mein Kampf*, Hitler portrayed his father as a lowly customs official who brought up his family in a state of near poverty. This was completely misleading. Alois Hitler carved out a very successful career as a well-paid official in the Imperial Customs Service. Between 1855 and 1895, he worked as a customs officer in several Austrian towns. He was frequently promoted, wore the grand uniform of a senior local Habsburg official and lived in affluent circumstances, enjoying a salary and a public status much higher than the headmaster of a secondary school. The idea of Adolf Hitler living in poverty as a child is even more misleading. He was a clean, well-dressed, provincial, middle-class boy who lived in affluent circumstances.

In Braunau am Inn, from 1889 to 1892, the family lived in a large, imposing home set in large and pretty grounds. The next home was a palatial apartment in Passau, Bavaria, where the family lived from 1892 to 1895. In 1895, Alois Hitler retired, with a very generous pension, and purchased a large country house, set in nine acres of land, in Hafeld, 30 miles outside Linz. In 1897, the family then went to live in the small rural town of Lambach, in a large third-floor apartment, opposite a Benedictine monastery. They stayed in Lambach for two years before moving on again to a pleasant house with a large garden in Leonding, a village on the outskirts of Linz.

All this moving around meant Hitler had to change schools frequently. At his first primary school, at Fischlam, near Lambach, he was popular with his schoolmates and gained good marks in all subjects. At his next school, in Leonding, he became withdrawn, sullen and moody; his marks slipped to below average, where they were to remain for the rest of his primary school career. In September 1900, aged 11, Hitler began his secondary education at the fee-paying *Realschule* in Linz, which specialised in preparing boys for a commercial, technical or civil service career. Hitler's journey to school involved a three-mile walk. At the *Realschule*, Hitler's marks fluctuated between 'good' and 'average'. He took very little interest in most subjects except history – where his teacher fired his imagination with stories of German nationalism – geography (he loved reading maps) and art, which was his greatest passion. His teachers remembered him as a resentful, moody and generally lazy pupil. It was while he was at the *Realschule* that Hitler claimed he became a fanatical German nationalist. His great German heroes were the soldier king Frederick the Great and Otto von Bismarck, the first German Chancellor.

Hitler at play as a child

Outside school, Hitler enjoyed playing imaginary war games and reading adventure stories. He often led his schoolmates in games of cowboys and Red Indians. Hitler always liked to play a Red Indian in these games; as underdogs, they appealed to him. He also greatly enjoyed reading the adventure stories about cowboys and Indians written by the German writer Karl May. Another passion was war comics. Hitler admitted that as a child he was 'enthusiastic about everything that was in any way connected with war'.[2] One of his favourite war games was to re-enact the Boer struggle against the British Empire. Hitler was once more on the side of the underdogs: the Boers. Indeed, he told friends he would like to enlist in the Boer army.

The death of his father

On 3 January 1903, Alois Hitler died of a lung haemorrhage. He was buried two days later in the cemetery in Leonding. The death of his father, no doubt inwardly traumatic, seems to have come as something of a relief to the young Adolf Hitler, who was now free of his father's tyrannical discipline and able to pursue his dream of becoming 'a great artist'. In economic terms, the Hitler family were placed in poorer circumstances, but nowhere near poverty. Klara received the property owned by her husband, a widow's pension, equivalent to 50 per cent of the income of the headmaster of a secondary school, and a substantial lump sum. Each child was left a lump sum and was entitled to 240 kronen per year until the age of 24.

Hitler as a youth

Shortly after his father's death, Hitler persuaded his mother to let him board in Linz, thus avoiding his long walk to school. He neglected his school work and had to pass re-sit examinations in each of his remaining years at secondary school. The headmaster at the *Realschule* at Linz, no doubt tired of Hitler's lack of effort, told him to take his final year at another *Realschule*, at Steyr, some 25 miles away. In effect, he had been expelled. Hitler stayed in lodgings in Steyr for his final year and passed his final re-sit examination. But to achieve the coveted school diploma (*Abitur*) required more schooling, at an *Oberrealschule*. Hitler could not face this, so he persuaded his mother to let him leave school in September 1905, aged 16. Hitler's self-inflicted failure at school left him with a lifelong contempt of book-learned academics and intellectuals.

After the death of her husband, Klara Hitler sold the house in Leonding and moved to Linz, renting a small flat in the town centre. At this stage in his life, Adolf Hitler showed no sign of being a future rabble-rousing dictator. He resembled a young Bohemian, with fairly long hair, a fashionable moustache and smart clothes.[3] He lived the life of a young dilettante: stayed in bed until noon and spent the afternoon going to cafés, art galleries and libraries. In the evening, he visited the opera (he particularly loved Wagner) with his close friend August Kubizek, a gifted young musician.[4]

In spite of all the superficial psychoanalysis which has been written about Hitler's childhood, it can be seen it was relatively stable and quite ordinary. Hitler showed no signs of mental instability or madness and gave no indication he would go on to become a messianic leader.

The death of his mother and the Vienna Academy

The most traumatic personal events in Hitler's teenage years were the death of his mother and his failure to gain entry to the Vienna Academy of Fine Arts. In January 1907, his mother became seriously ill with breast cancer. She underwent a mastectomy and seemed on the road to recovery. In the summer of 1907, Hitler persuaded his mother to allow him to withdraw his inheritance of 700 kronen and go to Vienna with the intention of gaining entry to the prestigious Academy of Fine Arts. For a school drop-out, without any qualifications, this was an overambitious plan. He rented a small flat in Vienna, took his examination for the Academy, but failed miserably. Never has history been so dramatically affected by the negative attitude of a small group of art lecturers to a few paintings. Of course, the lecturers in Vienna cannot be blamed for what came later, but their rejection of Hitler does illustrate how history can be altered by the most trivial matters. Hitler was astounded by his rejection, describing the examiners as 'fossilized Bureaucrats devoid of any understanding of young talent'.[5] But the examiners were right: Hitler was not a very good artist. His paintings and drawings from this period show he was technically competent at copying other people's work, but he lacked the ability to create original works of his own. He could paint buildings or landscapes, but not people. Art experts have suggested Hitler's style of painting does not reveal any deep psychological difficulty, certainly no psychopathic tendencies. Even his tendency to paint buildings is viewed as the product of an introverted personality, not deep mental difficulties.

In late October 1907, Hitler was given more depressing news – his mother's cancer was now terminal. He returned home to nurse his dying mother, night and day, very rarely leaving her bedside. But on 21 December 1907, she died; she was buried next to her husband in Leonding. According to Dr Bloch, the family physician: 'In all my career I have never seen anyone as prostrate with grief as Adolf Hitler.'[6] Hitler told Bloch, who was Jewish, 'I will be grateful to you for ever.' He kept his word. Bloch escaped persecution after the Nazis came to power.

Hitler's Vienna years, 1908–13

In February 1908, Hitler returned to Vienna, where he remained for the next five and a half years. In March 1908, he was joined by his close friend Kubizek, who had gained entry to the prestigious Vienna Academy of Music. They shared a flat for the next few months. During this time, Kubizek saw Hitler write poetry and attempt to write a play and an opera (set in Iceland). Hitler also visited the opera three nights a week. In the summer of 1908, Kubizek went home for the vacation. While he was away, Hitler tried once more to gain entry to the Academy of Fine Arts, in October 1908. He failed yet again. This second failure had a devastating effect, plunging Hitler into a deep depression. He decided to break all his links with the past. In November 1908, Kubizek returned to Vienna, but found Hitler had gone, leaving no forwarding address. It seems likely that Hitler could not face telling Kubizek, the only friend he had, about his failure.

Down and out in Vienna?

Hitler later described his time in Vienna as the saddest years of his life. He made no real effort to gain a proper job. He lived in three different flats from the autumn of 1908 to the late summer of 1909. Sometime in 1909, Hitler's financial position deteriorated, but exactly why it did remains difficult to explain. In the summer months of 1909, he did live rough, mostly sleeping on park benches. It is obvious that he was suffering from some sort of deep anxiety in this period, perhaps caused by his rejection by the Academy of Fine Arts. The brief, possibly self-inflicted experience as a 'down and out' in Vienna, which lasted less than three months, was greatly exaggerated by Hitler in *Mein Kampf*.

Hitler claimed he earned his daily bread as a labourer and by selling paintings in Vienna. There is no evidence of Hitler ever working as a labourer, but he did sell paintings. The very few people who knew him at this time recorded their views on him much later, thus distorting any understanding of what he was really like. Of course, they describe him as an opinionated, self-contained person, full of bright ideas, prejudices and grand plans, but seemingly too lazy to put in the effort to carry them out.

In October 1909, Hitler moved into the Meidling, a men's hostel, funded by a wealthy Jewish family. It was here that he was befriended by Reinhold Hanisch, an unemployed and street-wise domestic servant, originally from Berlin. Hanisch advised Hitler to write to his well-off relatives for some money to purchase artist's materials and then set himself up as a commercial artist. Hanisch promised to sell Hitler's paintings and postcards in return for a 50 per cent commission. Hitler wrote to his Aunt Johanna, who sent him 50 kronen, a sum Hanisch described as 'a nice piece of money in those days'. Hitler bought an overcoat and some artist's materials with the money.

Hitler moved to the Männerheim, a smart lodging house, mainly occupied by working men on limited incomes, in December 1909. The residents paid nearly three kronen a week for a small room. In return, they enjoyed access to many other facilities, including a large dining room, a reading room, a shower room and a laundry. Residents had to vacate their rooms during working hours, which meant that Hitler had to paint near a window in the lounge.

It is estimated that Hitler produced somewhere between 700 and 800 paintings, drawings and postcards between 1909 and 1913. The partnership between Hitler and Hanisch ended acrimoniously in 1910 when Hitler had Hanisch arrested on a charge of cheating him out of his share of a painting of the parliament building in Vienna. Hanisch spent eight days in jail for this offence. In

1936, Hanisch was arrested by the Gestapo, charged with spreading 'libellous stories about Hitler'. He died in Nazi custody on 4 February 1937, reportedly from a heart attack, but it is highly likely that he was murdered by the Gestapo. It never paid to double-cross Hitler.

At the end of 1910, Hitler's financial position greatly improved. It is estimated that he was earning 70 to 80 kronen a month from the sales of his paintings. This was supplemented by a substantial gift of perhaps 3,800 kronen from his Aunt Johanna. Another sign of his healthy financial state was his decision to transfer his orphan's pension to his half-sister, Angela. Indeed, Hitler was in great danger of exceeding the annual earnings limit of 1,400 kronen per annum imposed on residents at the Männerheim. He continued to stay there, not because he was poor, or needed to, but because it provided cheap accommodation, allowed him room to complete his artwork and prevented him from being in complete isolation.

Hitler's political ideas in Vienna

During Hitler's Vienna period, he certainly fits the description of a 'coffee house dreamer'. He saw himself as 'an artist' and took no active part in politics. In *Mein Kampf*, Hitler claimed that he was a very interested observer of politics and had monitored the appeal of three major parties of pre-1914 Vienna very closely: the Christian Socialists, led by Dr Karl Lüger (Mayor of Vienna); the Social Democratic Party; and the Pan-German Nationalists. Hitler greatly admired Dr Karl Lüger, a brilliant orator, who filled the ears of the lower middle classes with horror stories about the power of the Jews. The only shortcoming of Lüger, claimed Hitler, was his failure to champion German nationalism. Hitler had a 'great hatred' of the Social Democratic Party, because of its devotion to Marxist ideas, but he admired its ability to use propaganda to attract the masses and the willingness of its supporters to go out in the streets to fight for what they believed in. Hitler admits that he was most attracted by the nationalist ideas of the Pan-German Nationalist Party. The only problem with this party was its failure to appeal to the masses. Hitler claims the idea of combining extreme German nationalism, charismatic leadership and mass support in a new political party was already forming in his mind during his Vienna days. We only have Hitler's word that his political ideas were as clear as this before 1914. It is probably more accurate to suggest that these views about his Vienna period were self-serving rhetoric, designed to portray himself as a man of crystal-clear vision, when in all probability he took no more interest in politics than the average person in Vienna at the time.

The same is probably true of Hitler's explanation of his anti-Semitism. There is little evidence in Hitler's early life to suggest that ingrained prejudice against the Jews was a dominant preoccupation. The warm feelings Hitler expressed to Dr Bloch after his mother's death hardly indicate a congenital hatred of Jews. Hitler even admits he was tolerant of Jews when he arrived in Vienna. At this time, Hitler did not view Jews as a 'race' but as a religious group. He claims it was after reading anti-Semitic pamphlets and observing life in Vienna that he came to believe the Jews were a united race. 'Gradually,' claims Hitler, 'I had ceased to be a weak-kneed cosmopolitan and become an anti-Semite.'[7] In spite of these claims, there is no real evidence that a virulent anti-Semitism dominated Hitler's political thinking during his Vienna period. The anti-Semitic attitudes Hitler expressed at the time were fairly common and cannot be regarded as extreme or exceptional in the context of the times. In fact, he is known to have attended musical evenings at the home of a Jewish family; many of his friends at the Männerheim were Jewish; and he even preferred selling his paintings through Jewish art dealers because he regarded them as more honest. It seems that Hitler's anti-Semitism grew after 1918.

Hitler moves to Munich, 1913

In May 1913, Hitler suddenly ended his lonely and very unsuccessful period in Vienna. He travelled by train across the Austrian border to the modern city of Munich, Bavaria, southern Germany. Hitler's fateful relationship with Germany and its people had now begun. It was not his love of Germany which was the major reason for Hitler's hasty departure from Vienna. At the time, Hitler, who had already avoided conscription, feared that he was about to be called up for service with the Austrian army. Hitler later claimed he was a 'draft dodger', not out of cowardice, but because he did not want to join the Austrian army. On 20 January 1914, the Austrian authorities finally caught up with him in Munich and asked him to explain why he was avoiding military service. Hitler was forced to go to Salzburg to explain his actions. In February 1914, a military recruitment panel decided Adolf Hitler, future champion of the idea of a 'master race', was 'unfit for service' owing to a minor chest complaint.

Hitler describes his time in Munich before the First World War as the 'happiest and by far the most contented of my life'. He took lodgings with the family of Joseph Popp, a tailor, at a cost of 20 marks a month. The Popp family later described Hitler as leading a solitary existence in Munich. He read books, painted and spent lengthy periods in his room.

Hitler at war

In August 1914, when the First World War began, Hitler was in Munich. 'I am not ashamed to say,' Hitler later wrote, 'carried away by the enthusiasm of the moment, I sank down on my knees and thanked heaven out of the fullness of my heart for granting me the good fortune of being permitted to live in such a time.'[8] Hitler immediately volunteered to serve in the German army. He was accepted by the Bavarian List Regiment and spent most of the war carrying messages, often on a motorbike, between the officer staff and front-line troops.

Hitler's passionate involvement with the fate of the German army during the First World War was the real turning point in his life. His time in the army deeply intensified his extreme feelings of German nationalism. Hitler describes his period in the German army as 'the most memorable period of my life'. He was a very good soldier, receiving the Iron Cross, second class, in August 1914, and the Iron Cross, first class, in August 1918, a bravery award rarely given to a volunteer. (The latter award was given on the recommendation of a Jewish officer.) The highest rank Hitler achieved was lance-corporal, but there is no evidence that he had any aspirations for promotion to the rank of non-commissioned officer.

Hitler was viewed as somewhat eccentric by the other soldiers. He never requested leave, nor received any letters from home. Some fellow soldiers found his unquestioning, unflinching patriotism towards the German cause somewhat irritating. Hitler was seriously wounded in the leg at the Battle of the Somme in 1916 and briefly blinded in a mustard gas attack in October 1918. He was in hospital recovering from the attack when he heard news of Germany's defeat: 'Everything went black again before my eyes; I tottered and groped my way back to the ward, threw myself on my bunk, and dug my burning head into my blanket and pillow. So it had all been in vain.'[9]

This was a deeply significant moment in Hitler's political awakening. He believed that Germany was not defeated in battle, but 'stabbed in the back by socialists, Jews and democratic politicians'. The Weimar Republic was never accepted as legitimate by Hitler. When the new government signed the controversial Treaty of Versailles on 28 June 1919, the idea of Germany being betrayed by the new democratic government became widespread among the nationalist right. Among the terms of Versailles were: a reduction of the German army to 100,000, the loss of 13 per cent of German territory and all its colonies and the payment of £6.6 billion in reparations.

The early growth of the Nazi Party

In November 1918, Hitler returned to Munich, but remained in the army. Munich was in a state of unprecedented political crisis. The king of Bavaria was deposed in a socialist revolution. Kurt Eisner, a Jewish Social Democrat, set up the Bavarian People's Republic, but he was assassinated in February 1919 by a renegade army officer. This incident provoked a workers' revolt, which led to the creation of a workers' republic. This did not last long. In April 1919, troops supported by the free corps (*Freikorps*), consisting of hundreds of patriotic, trigger-happy ex-soldiers, crushed the workers' revolt. A moderate Social Democrat government was put back in power, but this was soon replaced by an extreme right-wing nationalist administration led by Gustav von Kahr.

During the Weimar period, Bavaria was a citadel for right-wing nationalists. The Bavarian right consisted of four elements: the regular army (*Reichswehr*), monarchists, national conservatives and a mob of right-wing ex-soldiers. They all shared a hatred of Bolshevism and a burning desire to overthrow the Weimar Republic. Bavaria – one of the most independent of the German federal states – was thus an ideal place to form an extreme nationalist party with the aim of overthrowing the Weimar Republic.[10] Hitler was now in the right place at the right time. He gave his support in the early post-war years to those elements within

9

the German army who wanted to crush the left and overthrow the Republic by force; in turn, these groups aided Hitler's rise to political prominence in Bavarian politics.

Hitler's exact relationship with the German army in Bavaria from 1918 to 1923 is still shrouded in mystery. Hitler was picked out by Captain Karl May – no doubt because of his unquestioning patriotic loyalty – to become a 'political instructor' in the Press and Political Bureau of the army. It was because of his selection as a 'political instructor' by his army superiors that Hitler began to realise that he was a very talented public speaker. In June 1919, he was sent by the army on a short course on 'anti-Bolshevism' at Munich University. This was designed to prepare him for his new role as an army spy and propagandist.

Hitler's first major assignment was to investigate the numerous right- and left-wing groups which were agitating for revolution in Munich. One group Hitler was recommended to observe was the German Workers' Party (*Deutsche Arbeiterpartei*, or DAP), set up by Anton Drexler, a Munich locksmith, in March 1919. Drexler wanted to build a political party that combined an extreme nationalist line with some socialist ideas designed to weaken the appeal of Marxism among workers.

The DAP had less than 40 members and held its meetings in Munich beer halls. On 12 September 1919, Hitler went to observe and speak at a meeting of the DAP, attended by about 20 people. He claims his speech at the meeting left such a favourable impression on Drexler that he was immediately asked to join the DAP committee, as only its seventh member. Already on the committee was Captain Ernst Röhm, a member of the army's district command in Munich and certainly someone Hitler must have already known. Also on the committee was Gottfried Feder, who had lectured Hitler on the course on anti-Bolshevism at Munich University. These links suggest that the army was already thinking of using the DAP's novel combination of nationalism and socialism as a vehicle for its own anti-Marxist propaganda.

Hitler, with a little help from his army friends, quickly replaced Drexler as the leading orator and propagandist in the party. On 24 February 1920, the DAP changed its name to the National Socialist German Workers' Party (*Nationalsozialistische Deutsche Arbeiterpartei*, or NSDAP), commonly known as the Nazi Party. It was actually Hitler who designed the distinctive and now universally familiar swastika symbol, used on party propaganda, party flags and the distinctive Nazi armbands.

On 1 April 1920, Hitler decided to leave the army, with the intention of championing its aims in a different uniform. In December 1920, the unknown NSDAP purchased a weekly newspaper, the *Münchener Beobachter*, for 180,000 marks, and renamed it the *Völkischer Beobachter* (*People's Observer*). The money to buy the paper came from Dietrich Eckart (who provided Hitler and the party with useful and wealthy contacts), from various prominent Munich conservatives and from army secret funds (60,000 marks).

Hitler assembled around him in Munich a group of key figures in the early Nazi movement. Alfred Rosenberg, self-styled party philosopher, provided a great deal of the racial theories of the party, especially its marked anti-Semitic views.[11] Max Amann, Hitler's former army sergeant, became publishing manager of the party. Ernst Röhm, a tough and menacing bully boy, recruited thousands of ex-soldiers and members of the paramilitary Freikorps to form the storm troopers (*Stormabteilungen*, or SA), a private army which grew into a fearsome street fighting force. Röhm also helped Hitler to solidify his links with prominent army figures. Hermann Göring, a highly decorated fighter pilot, introduced Hitler to many important figures in Bavarian high society. Another very important early recruit was Rudolf Hess, who had been awarded the Iron Cross, first class, had been in Hitler's own regiment and was obviously a loyal friend of Hitler's. From the very beginning, the Nazi Party's motto could have been 'show us your war medals'.

Indeed, so many ex-soldiers were involved in the early Nazi Party, it is probably best described as an army propaganda unit, led by an extreme nationalist, supported by a paramilitary private army ready and willing to overthrow the state. Even the organisation of the early NSDAP resembled the command structure of the army. The leader had complete control over the party (known as the *Führerprinzip* – leadership principle). Every member was expected to follow the will of the leader without comment or discussion. Any party member who wished to alter the party programme faced immediate expulsion.

The early programme of the Nazi Party

In February 1920, the 25-point party programme of the NSDAP was drawn up by Gottfried Feder. The chief gimmick of the Nazi Party was to combine essentially right-wing, nationalist and anti-Semitic ideas with some limited anti-capitalist, so-called 'socialist' measures. The 'national' elements of the programme included revision of the Treaty of Versailles, the union of all German speakers into a Greater German Reich, the exclusion of Jews from citizenship rights, state control of the press and a strong totalitarian state led by an all-powerful dictator. The 'socialist' parts of the programme included promises to nationalise trusts, abolish land rents, restrict interest on loans, introduce profit sharing in industry, open up department stores to small traders, confiscate profits made by industry during war and create a people's army based on the SA.

The 'nationalist' parts of the party programme were not substantially different from those of other extreme nationalist groups, but they were genuinely believed in and supported by Hitler, who implemented most of them after he became Chancellor. What distinguished the NSDAP from other fringe groups on the nationalist right was its advocacy of certain 'socialist' policies. The 'socialist' elements of the party programme were genuinely supported by a radical section within the party, but were viewed by Hitler as largely window dressing, designed to attract support from the workers. Very few of the 'socialist' elements of the party programme were ever carried out by Hitler when he came to power. It must be understood that Hitler was quite willing to use the slogans and symbols of socialism in order to gain support for his own brand of extreme nationalism.

The Munich beer hall putsch

The most significant event in the early history of the Nazi Party was the bungled Munich beer hall putsch, which took place in November 1923 when Hitler, accompanied by 600 members of the SA, attempted to seize power in Munich.[12] It was planned by Hitler in conjunction with renegade forces in the army, most notable among whom was General Ludendorff. On 8 November 1923, von Kahr, the leader of the Bavarian government, was addressing a group of prominent government officials and businessmen in a large beer hall in Munich when Hitler, accompanied by a large number of SA men, burst in. Hitler, wearing a rather shabby overcoat, jumped onto a table, fired a shot from a revolver into the ceiling and shouted to the assembled audience in a rather hoarse voice: 'The National Revolution has begun.' Yet the three groups Hitler expected to join his march on Berlin to overthrow the government – the army, the police and the Bavarian government – all refused to offer support. This left Hitler and the Nazi Party completely isolated. The following day, Hitler, accompanied by a group of 300 armed storm troopers, marched towards the centre of Munich, intending to capture the War Ministry, but they were met by the police, who killed 16 members of the SA and easily crushed the revolt.

The Munich beer hall putsch was a bungled and humiliating failure. It was very poorly planned. There was no liaison with leading figures in the Bavarian government or with other right-wing groups. Even worse, there was no concerted plan of action for a seizure of power or a march on Berlin. Hitler was

February 1924. The leading members of the putsch before their trial. Ludendorff and Hitler are centre right, and Röhm is standing second from the right.

arrested, tried and convicted of high treason. He received the very lenient sentence of five years in prison, the minimum possible, but served only 13 months in Landsberg prison. At this time, Hitler's meteoric rise in Bavarian politics seemed to be over. However, Hitler used his time in prison in two very constructive ways. First, he decided to transform the Nazi Party into a major national political party, which would contest democratic elections and then destroy democracy with a legal revolution after gaining power. Second, Hitler decided to set out a clear set of political ideas for the party in a book which he hoped would become a bible for his followers.

Hitler's ideology and aims

The book which Hitler wrote while locked up in Landsberg prison was called *Mein Kampf* (*My Struggle*). There are many language errors in *Mein Kampf*, which ran to 752 pages. It is written in a very ponderous style, full of long words which the author appears not to know how to use properly. Even so, *Mein Kampf* is extremely important because it outlines Hitler's view of Germany under his own leadership, the fundamental principles of his *Weltanschauung* (world view, or ideology) and his key foreign policy objectives.[13]

Hitler's first objective was 'complete dominance over the country by the leaders of the movement'. To gain power, Hitler was prepared to be pragmatic and flexible. The use of propaganda was viewed as a crucial weapon in winning mass support. Hitler believed the masses could be duped into supporting just about any policy if 'the same message was repeated over and over again'. In Hitler's view, the great mass of voters 'will more easily fall victim to a great lie than to a small one'.

The question of race is another dominant theme of the book. Hitler viewed life as a struggle for existence between the strong and pure races and the weak and mixed ones. War was a key part of this struggle, in which the strongest and purest race would dominate. The question of how Germany was to become the strongest race occupied a great deal of Hitler's attention. He divided the world into three racial groups: 'Aryans' – defined as those races who create cultures; the 'bearers of culture' – classed as those races who cannot create culture, but who can copy from Aryans; and 'inferior peoples' – defined as having no capacity to create culture, or copy from others, being capable only of destroying cultures. The key objective of Hitler's racial policy was to create a pure Aryan race of Germans, which would not 'weaken its blood' by having children with people of different races. If a racially pure, thoroughbred group of Germans could be created, then Hitler believed it would be 'the highest species of humanity on this earth'.

The type of society Hitler wanted to create was a popular folk community (*Volksgemeinschaft*). The idea of creating a folk community was a very popular and nostalgic idea among all sections of the German nationalist right. It denoted a return to a primitive rural form of society based on 'blood and soil' and it romanticised Germany's medieval past. According to Hitler, the rural harmony between knights and peasants was shattered by the rise of the bourgeoisie, by modern industrial society and by Marxism. Hence, the way forward was to take Germany backwards, to a rural lifestyle in which each German could live on the land.

The type of government for such a folk community would be an authoritarian one, with no majority decisions and no democratic votes – one in which everything was decided 'by one man' and an 'elite of leaders'. The leader (*Führer*) would give orders downwards, which were expected to be obeyed. The individual in such a society was expected to follow these orders without question or discussion. The future Nazi state would not promote equality, only equality of opportunity. Hitler defined the folk community as a classless society in which individuals would find their own natural level through hard work, willpower and effort. A future Nazi state would seek to remove class barriers, but would accept there would be differences among individuals in talent, status and wealth. Indeed, Hitler suggested the Nazi state would promote the 'victory of the better and stronger and demand the subordination of the inferior and the weaker'.[14] Hitler was extremely vague about where 'socialism' came into his proposed folk community. He defined his brand of 'socialism' in the following way:

> Whoever is prepared to make the national cause his own to such an extent that he knows no higher ideal than the welfare of his nation; whoever has understood our great national anthem, 'Deutschland ueber Alles' to mean that nothing in the wide world surpasses in his eyes this Germany, people and land – that man is a socialist.[15]

According to this definition, Hitler's 'socialism' is really a form of blind national patriotism.

The key enemies barring the way to Hitler's racially pure folk community were Marxists and Jews. Hitler had a burning, indeed obsessive and passionate, hatred of Marxism. It runs through all his writings and speeches. But whenever Hitler spoke of Marxists, he implied they were all 'Jews' or 'controlled by Jews'. To a very great extent, Hitler's anti-Marxism was interwoven with his anti-Semitism. He defined Jews not as a religious group but as a united race. The Jews, claimed Hitler, were planning a world conspiracy, supposedly outlined in 'The Protocols of Zion', a forged document which outlined a Zionist desire for Jewish world domination. Hitler implied that because the Jews were stateless (the state of Israel was not established until 1948), they undermined the ethnic unity of every state they lived in. Hitler believed every corrupting influence was Jewish in origin. Jews were described by Hitler in *Mein Kampf* as 'not human', 'vermin', 'parasites' and 'germs'. He wanted to 'eliminate' Jews from German society.

Anti-Semitism had two functions within Nazi ideology. It provided a simple explanation for all the divisions and problems in German society, and suggested that a full solution to those ills could be achieved only by eliminating Jews from German society and then by eliminating Jews in the country most dominated by 'Jewish Bolshevism' – the Soviet Union.

But the greatest amount of space in *Mein Kampf* is devoted to Hitler's foreign policy aims. The first of these was to 'abolish the Treaty of Versailles', but this was only the first stage in a resurgence of German militarism of a more extreme variety. 'To demand [only] that the 1914 frontiers of Germany be restored,' wrote Hitler in *Mein Kampf*, 'is a political absurdity.'[16] To begin with, Hitler wanted to extend German territory by including all German speakers in Austria and the Sudetenland (a region of Czechoslovakia) into a greater German Reich. Hitler realised the achievement of this aim would be opposed by France and a war with France was always implicit in his foreign policy thinking. Hitler wanted to persuade Britain to abandon its long-standing support for upholding a balance of power in Europe and give Germany a 'free hand' to establish continental hegemony.

The most dominant aim of Hitler's foreign policy was to gain *Lebensraum* (living space) in eastern Europe. This implied a war of conquest against Soviet Russia. The ultimate aim of *Lebensraum* was to provide enough living space to create a German population explosion, which would eventually create a Greater German Reich of 250 million 'racially pure' Germans, self-sufficient in food and raw materials, a dominant European superpower.

The great difficulty for historians is to decide whether Hitler's ideas were a blueprint for action or a dream. Any set of plans is always limited by structural restraints and the opportunity and willingness to carry them out. But we should not underestimate Hitler's willpower and determination to carry out many of his key foreign policy aims. It is, therefore, very hard to reject the notion that Hitler's ideas did amount to a framework for action, pursued as a set of objectives. When Hitler did improvise or compromise his aims, it was nearly always for a tactical reason and did not lead him to abandon any fundamental objectives. It seems reasonable to suggest that Hitler, if he was able, aimed to destroy German democracy, build up German military strength, overthrow the Treaty of Versailles, absorb German speakers in Austria and Czechoslovakia, gain living space in eastern Europe at the expense of the Soviet Union and at the very least 'eliminate' all Jews from German society.

Hitler's rise to power

Ideology alone cannot fully explain Hitler's rise to power. The appointment of Hitler in January 1933 was not due to overwhelming electoral support. The highest percentage of votes ever recorded for the NSDAP before 1933 was 37.4 per cent, in July 1932. When Hitler was given power in a coalition government by President Hindenburg in 1933, Nazi support was actually slipping. Any discussion of Hitler's rise to power must focus on the following three factors: the vulnerability of democracy in Weimar Germany under President Hindenburg; the collapse of the German economy from 1929 onwards; and the rapid growth of support for the Nazi Party.

The vulnerability of Weimar democracy

The democratic system in Germany between 1919 and 1933 did not have widespread support. The Weimar Republic (named after the town where its new democratic constitution was agreed) was saddled with a heavy burden of responsibility for the national humiliation which followed military defeat in the First World War. Somewhere along the way, the idea that German militarism was the real culprit for the German predicament after 1918 seems to have been submerged beneath nationalist rhetoric. The 'stab in the back' myth proved a useful rallying call to the opponents of Weimar democracy.[17]

There were many flaws within the Weimar constitution. The voting system was organised on the basis of proportional representation, which encouraged weak coalition governments (in fact no single party ever commanded a majority) and allowed extreme parties a voice in the parliament (Reichstag). From 1919 to 1923, the infant republic survived being overthrown only because of the loyalty of the army and the police. There were a number of political parties on the extreme left and right which never accepted the legitimacy of the new republic.

In addition, article 48 of the constitution gave the President the power to ignore the wishes of the Reichstag and to use emergency powers to choose a government with no democratic majority. The first Weimar President, Friedrich Ebert, who ruled from 1918 to 1925, used article 48 sparingly, with the aim of sustaining democracy, but Paul von Hindenburg, President from 1925 to 1934, used it frequently, in a manner which completely undermined the power of the Reichstag and democracy. Hindenburg drew his support in the 1925 presidential election from a coalition of nationalists, the army, the Junkers (the land-owning German aristocracy) and some factions in heavy industry, but in the 1932 presidential election, socialists and Catholics supported Hindenburg in order to prevent Hitler taking power. In March 1930, the most stable coalition government, based on collaboration between the Social Democratic Party, the Deutsche Volkspartei and the Catholic Centre Party, fell apart.

From March 1930 to January 1933 each German Chancellor was chosen by Hindenburg and kept in power using article 48 of the constitution. This gave the impression of Germany being in a perpetual state of political crisis. In March 1930, Hindenburg appointed Heinrich Brüning, a member of the Catholic Centre Party, as the Chancellor of a 'national government'. He introduced a bleak set of deflationary policies, which included public expenditure cuts and tax increases. The result was to make the economic depression worse and increase unemployment further.

In March 1932, Hindenburg forced the increasingly unpopular Brüning to resign, replacing him with Franz von Papen, another leading figure of the Catholic Centre Party, with close links to the aristocracy and the army, but little support in the Reichstag. Von Papen immediately declared a 'state of emergency' and suspended the Prussian parliament, the stronghold of the Social Democratic Party. The von Papen regime, dubbed 'the cabinet of barons', was driven out of office by a vote of no confidence in the Reichstag in November 1932. By this time, parliamentary government had virtually collapsed. During 1932, for example, the Reichstag met only 13 times. In December 1932, Hindenburg appointed a leading army figure – General von Schleicher – as Chancellor, but he lasted a mere 57 days. It was on 30 January 1933 that Hindenburg, under the influence of leading business and army figures, finally decided to invite Adolf Hitler to form a national coalition government. Hitler was 'invited' into office by President Hindenburg to establish a stable right-wing authoritarian dictatorship, upholding the aims of the army, the agrarian Junkers and big business. It was hoped Hitler could be harnessed to serve the needs of the old guard. During 1932, Hitler had assiduously courted army and business leaders. In January 1932, Hitler told a meeting of leading German industrialists in Düsseldorf they had nothing to fear from the radicals in the NSDAP. The leading radicals in the Nazi Party were incensed by what they regarded as Hitler's abandonment of his 'socialist' ideals. At the end of 1932, Gregor Strasser, leader of the social revolutionary north German wing of the party and Hitler's most dangerous party rival, resigned from the Nazi Party, outraged at what he saw as Hitler's growing alliance with the old guard and big business. This rift helped Hitler to convince the old guard he was abandoning the radicals in favour of the traditional German establishment. The old guard wanted the new government to pass an enabling law that would make the enactment of laws dependent on the cabinet and not the Reichstag. It was assumed that, as the new cabinet was dominated by a conservative, non-Nazi majority, the old right would be able to tame and control Hitler. What the old guard could not predict was how Hitler would use the enabling law to set up a one-party state, and destroy all independent political parties. The old guard had wanted Weimar democracy destroyed on its terms and failed to see that Hitler, once given power, would destroy it on his.

The role of economic factors

The second factor which greatly aided the growth of support for the Nazi Party was the impact of the world depression on the German economy.[18] The background to many of the political difficulties of the Weimar period was severe economic problems. From 1919 to 1923, a deeply unstable political period, the German mark went into free fall as inflation rose high. The 'great inflation' of 1923 left many Germans bankrupt, with millions losing savings and pensions. It undermined the stability of the *Mittelstand* (middle class), leaving a deep reservoir of economic discontent. The period from 1924 to 1929 witnessed a partial economic recovery and gave some hope that Germany's miserable economic plight might be over. This optimism was shattered by the monumental collapse of the German economy after 1929. The German recovery in the mid-1920s had been greatly aided by US loans, which dried up in the aftermath of the Wall Street Crash in October 1929. After this financial collapse, unemployment soared from 1.4 million in 1928 to nearly 6 million in 1932. Industrial production fell by 42 per cent and the farming community in rural Germany was heavily hit. It was in the midst of the 'Great Depression' that support for the Nazi Party grew. It seems the economic collapse which occurred after 1929 intensified feelings against the Weimar Republic and thereby paved the way to the collapse of democracy.

The growth in electoral support for the Nazi Party

The final factor which brought Hitler to power was the growth in electoral support for the Nazi Party from 2.6 per cent of voters in 1928 to 37.3 per cent in 1932. A great deal of this remarkable transformation was due to Adolf Hitler's leadership. The failure of the Munich beer hall putsch and his period in jail changed Hitler from an incompetent street fighter into a shrewd and skilful politician. He decided the road to power lay not through force alone, but by building a national movement. After his release from prison, Hitler quickly re-established total control over the party and turned it into a truly national party.

There has been a great deal of research on the growth of Nazi electoral support.[19] Nazi voting strength was much higher in Protestant areas than in Catholic regions. The Nazis could never weaken support for the Catholic Centre Party or the Bavarian People's Party in Catholic areas. The major electoral advances for the Nazi Party from 1930 to 1932 were in rural Protestant areas, usually at the expense of the German National People's Party and of small, right-wing, special-interest parties. The Nazis gained support in rural areas from agricultural labourers, farmers, peasants and landowners. The Nazis always made more substantial gains where they did not face strong traditional religious or ideological loyalties to other parties. The romantic idea of a folk community, coupled with promises to help farmers, seems to have been a vital contributory factor in the growth of Nazi support in rural areas.

The Nazi Party did far less well among electors in large cities and industrial areas. In July 1932, for example, support for the NSDAP in cities with a population of over 100,000 was 10 per cent lower than elsewhere. The Nazis found it difficult to attract support from workers in industry. Members of the working class who voted Nazi came predominantly from villages with a population of less than 5,000. The hard core of Nazi support in the 1930 Reichstag election came from the lower 'old' middle class in rural Protestant areas: small shopkeepers, independent artisans, farmers and agricultural labourers. By the July 1932 Reichstag election, however, the Nazis also drew support from the 'new' middle class: white-collar workers, upper-middle-class Protestants in the affluent suburbs and professionals, including teachers, doctors, civil servants and engineers. It seems many of these voters were attracted by the idea of a return to the 'golden days' before democracy had been introduced.

The most vexed question concerning the growth of Nazi electoral support is whether Hitler appealed to the working class.[20] In July 1932, the Nazi Party gained 25 per cent of the working-class vote. It has also been estimated that 55 per cent of storm troopers and 40 per cent of party members came from the working class. But the majority of Nazi working-class support came from rural labourers and workers in small-scale craft and domestic industries, who did not belong to trade unions. The Nazi Party failed to win substantial support from trade union members and industrial workers, who generally remained loyal to the Communist Party and the Social Democrats. More surprising, perhaps, is the failure of the Nazi Party to gain substantial support from the unemployed. In areas with the highest concentrations of unemployed industrial workers the Communist Party enjoyed over 60 per cent of the vote.

Nevertheless, it is now generally accepted that the Nazi Party attracted a broader spectrum of support than any other German political party in the Weimar period. By July 1932, the Nazi Party was the largest in the Reichstag. The limits of Hitler's electoral appeal, however, were very effectively illustrated during the 1932 presidential election. Hitler gained four times as many votes as Ernst Thälmann, the Communist Party candidate, but he lost decisively to President Hindenburg – by 19.4 million to 13.4 million votes. In the November 1932 Reichstag election, those who opposed the Nazi Party represented 63 per cent of the German electorate. In that same election, the Nazi Party lost 2 million votes and had clearly passed its peak. Even so, the growth of Nazi Party electoral support from 1930 to 1932 was a significant factor in Hitler's rise to power, because it placed the Nazi leader in a very good position to lead a right-wing authoritarian government. By turning the Nazi Party into the most popular German political party, the voters had helped Hitler to use his political skills to put pressure on Hindenburg to make him Chancellor.

Hitler's rise to power

1.1 Hitler's view on the ideology of National Socialism, 1928

I am a German nationalist. That is to say I am true to my nation. All my thoughts and actions are dedicated to it. I am a socialist. I recognise no class or status group, but rather a community of people, tied by blood, united by language, subject to a comprehensive fate. I love the nation and hate only its present ruling majority parties, because I regard them as unrepresentative of my nation.

Source: G. L. Weinberg (ed.), *Hitler's Zweites Buch. Ein Dokument aus dem Jahr 1928*, Stuttgart, 1969, p. 69

1.2 Hitler claims the Nazi Party opposes class conflict, 1930

The NSDAP is an organisation which does not recognise proletarians, does not recognise bourgeois, farmers, manual workers and so on; instead it is an organisation based on all regions of Germany, composed of all social groups. If you ask one of us; 'Young man, what are you? Bourgeois? Proletarian?', he will smile; 'I am German! I fight in my brown shirt.' That is indicative of our significance; we do not aspire to be anything else, we are all fighting for the future of a people. We are equal in our ranks.

Source: Speech in Kiel, 31 August 1930, Bundesarchiv, Koblenz, NS26/57

1.3 Hitler on the power of the mass meeting, 1925

Mass assemblies are necessary because whilst attending them the individual feels on the point of joining a young movement . . . submits himself to the magic influence of what we call 'mass suggestion'. The desires, longings, and indeed the strength of thousands is accumulated in the mind of each individual present. A man who enters such a meeting in doubt and hesitation, leaves it inwardly fortified; he has become a member of a community. The National Socialist Movement may never ignore this.

Source: A. Hitler, *Mein Kampf*, London, 1938, pp. 191–92

1.4 Gregor Strasser explains why people become National Socialists, 1927

Before the war we did not bother with politics . . . In the war we became nationalists, that is to say out of that vague feeling that the fatherland had to be defended, that it was something great and sacred, the protector of the existence of the individual, out of this vague notion which for us was not clear, we became nationalists on the battlefield . . . we could not help coming home with the brutal intention of gathering the whole nation around us and teaching them that the greatness of a nation depends on the willingness of the individual to stand up for the nation and say to it: Your fate is indissolubly linked with the fate of your people, with the fate and greatness of your nation. We could not help coming home from the war with this resolve: Those who have fought together with us and who are hostile towards the nation because it has not bothered with them must be emancipated so that Germany will in future be strong and the master of her enemies!

Source: J. Noakes and G. Pridham, *Documents on Nazism 1919–1945*, London, 1974, pp. 71–72

1.5 Joseph Goebbels explains the impact of Hitler's speeches on his followers, 1922

Like a rising star you appeared before our wondering eyes, you performed miracles to clear our minds, and in a world of scepticism and desperation, gave us faith. You towered above the masses, full of faith and certain of the future, and possessed by the will to free those masses with your unlimited love for all those who believe in the new Reich. For the first time we saw with shining eyes a man who tore off the mask from the faces distorted by greed, the faces of mediocre parliamentary busybodies . . . What you said are the greatest words spoken in Germany since Bismarck . . . We thank you. One day, Germany will thank you.

Source: W. Shirer, *The rise and fall of the Third Reich*, London, 1960, pp. 161–62

1.6 Hitler attacks coalition governments, 1925

It ought never to be forgotten that no really great achievement has ever been effected in this world by coalitions; instead they have always been due to the triumph of one individual man. Successes achieved by coalitions, owing to the nature of their source, contain the seeds of future disintegration . . . The national state, therefore, will never be created by the unstable national confederation of workers, but only by the . . . will-power of a single movement, after that movement has won through, having defeated all others.

Source: A. Hitler, *Mein Kampf*, London, 1938, p. 206

1.7 Hitler is questioned by Strasser on the issue of 'socialism', 1930

Strasser: You want to strangle the social revolution for the sake of legality and your new collaboration with the bourgeois parties of the right.

Hitler: I am a socialist . . . I would not allow my chauffeur to eat worse than I eat myself. But your kind of socialism is nothing but Marxism. The mass of the working classes want nothing but bread and games. They will never understand the meaning of an ideal, and we cannot hope to win them over to one . . . What you [Strasser] preach is liberalism, nothing but liberalism. There is only one possible kind of revolution, and it is not economic or political or social but racial . . . All revolutions – and I have studied them carefully – have been racial.

Strasser: Let us assume you come to power tomorrow. What would you do about Krupp's [a major German industry]? Would you leave it alone?

Hitler: Of course I should leave it alone . . . Do you think me so crazy as to want to ruin Germany's great industry?

Strasser: If you wish to preserve the capitalist regime, Herr Hitler, you have no right to talk of socialism.

Hitler: That word 'socialism' is the trouble . . . I have never said that all enterprises should be socialised . . . Our National Socialist state, like the Fascist state [in Italy], will safeguard both employers' and workers' interests.

Source: Interview between Strasser and Hitler, 1930, quoted in J. Noakes and G. Pridham, *Documents on Nazism 1919–1945*, London, 1974, pp. 99–100

1.8 Von Papen speaks on the 'German crisis', 1932

The German problem is the central problem of all the world's difficulties.

The German situation is characterized by the following:
1. The high level of interest, which crushes agriculture and also industry.
2. The burden of taxation, which is so oppressive.
3. The external debt.
4. Unemployment, which is relatively more widespread than in any other country whatever, and constitutes from 20 to 25 per cent of the population is a burden on public funds.

What is particularly fatal is that an ever-growing number of young people have no possibility of finding employment and earning their livelihood. Despair and the political radicalization of the youthful section of the population are the consequences of this state of things.

Source: S. Pollard and C. Holmes (eds.), *Documents of European history. The end of Old Europe 1914–1939, Vol. 3*, London, 1973, pp. 329–31

1.9 Otto Meissner, secretary to President Hindenburg, reports on the views of German business to the possible appointment of Hitler as Chancellor

I talked to a number of businessmen . . . The general desire of businessmen was to see a strong man come to power in Germany who would form a government that would stay in power for a long time. When the NSDAP suffered its first setback on 6 November 1932 [in the Reichstag election] and had thereby passed its peak, the need for support from German business became particularly urgent. Business had a common interest in the fear of Bolshevism and in the hope the National Socialists, once in power, would create lasting political and economic foundations in Germany. Another common interest was the wish to put Hitler's economic programme into practice, one of the main points of which was that business should manage its own affairs . . . Furthermore, big state orders were expected to achieve economic improvement.

Source: J. Noakes and G. Pridham, *Documents on Nazism 1919–1945*, London, 1974, pp. 146–47

Document case-study questions

1 Offer a brief definition of National Socialism, using evidence from 1.1 and 1.2.

2 Explain briefly what Hitler thinks about his potential supporters in 1.3.

3 Identify in 1.4 the major group Strasser believes National Socialism sought to appeal to.

4 What impression of Goebbel's view of Hitler can be gained from 1.5?

5 Is it possible to predict how Hitler would govern from his comments expressed in 1.6?

6 Assess briefly the differing views of Hitler and Strasser towards National Socialism expressed in 1.7 and briefly account for those differences.

7 What does von Papen view as the major problem facing Germany in 1.8?

8 Comment briefly on the attitude of German business towards the appointment of Hitler as Chancellor in 1933 as outlined in 1.9.

Notes and references

1 R. Waite, *The psychopathic god: Adolf Hitler*, New York, 1977, p. 137.

2 J. Toland, *Adolf Hitler*, London, 1976, p. 16.

3 For a useful evaluation of Hitler's early years see F. Jetzinger, *Hitler's youth*, London, 1958.

4 See A. Kubizek, *Young Hitler. The story of our friendship*, London, 1973.

5 Adolf Hitler, *Mein Kampf*, London, 1938, p. 20.

6 Toland, *Hitler*, p. 36.

7 W. Shirer, *The rise and fall of the Third Reich*, London, 1960, p. 43.

8 *Ibid.*, p. 46.

9 *Ibid.*

10 For a detailed discussion of the birth of the Nazi Party see G. Franz, 'Munich: Birthplace and center of the National Socialist German Workers' Party', *Journal of Modern History*, vol. 29 (1957).

11 Rosenberg was very influential in setting the violently anti-Semitic tone of the early Nazi Party. See R. Cecil, *The myth of the master race. Alfred Rosenberg and Nazi ideology*, London, 1972.

12 See H. Gordon, *Hitler and the beer hall putsch*, New York, 1972.

13 For a useful set of documents on Nazi ideology see B. M. Lane and L. J. Rupp (eds.), *Nazi ideology before 1933. A documentation*, Manchester, 1978.

14 Shirer, *Third Reich*, p. 118.

15 *Ibid.*, p. 114.

16 Hitler, *Mein Kampf*, p. 529.

17 See I. Kershaw (ed.), *Weimar. Why did German democracy fail?*, London, 1990.

18 See R. Evans and D. Geary (eds.), *The German unemployed. Experiences and consequences of mass unemployment from the Weimar Republic to the Third Reich*, London, 1987.

19 For a detailed discussion see T. Childers, *The Nazi voter*, London, 1983.

20 See C. Fischer (ed.), *Weimar, the working class and the rise of national socialism*, Oxford, 1995.

The Nazi state and economy

The consolidation of power, 1933–34

Adolf Hitler was appointed German Chancellor on 30 January 1933. There were only two other Nazis in the 11-strong coalition cabinet: Hermann Göring, Minister without Portfolio, and Wilhelm Frick, Minister of the Interior. The new government was dominated by the conservative old guard, most notably Alfred Hugenberg, leader of the German National People's Party, Franz von Papen, the former Chancellor, and General Werner von Blomberg, the War Minister. 'In two months,' von Papen confided to a friend, 'we'll have pushed Hitler into a corner, and he can squeal to his heart's content.'[1] Yet the old guard underestimated Hitler's political skill. From the very beginning, Hitler intended to break up the coalition and transform Germany into a one-party Nazi state.

The final democratic election campaign, 1933

Hitler's very first act as German Chancellor was to call for fresh elections on 5 March 1933. Hitler expected the Nazi Party to win an outright majority. Big business donated 3 million marks to finance the Nazi election campaign. Opposition parties faced an uphill struggle: Communist Party meetings were banned and the election rallies of the Social Democrats were broken up by the SA, which also disrupted meetings of the Catholic Centre Party. It was a very violent campaign, with 50 anti-Nazis and 18 Nazis killed in street clashes.

The Reichstag fire

The most dramatic event of the campaign occurred on 27 February 1933, when the Reichstag building was burned down. The police were on the scene in minutes, but did not call the fire brigade for a full half hour. They did manage to arrest a young unemployed Dutch Communist – Marinus van der Lubbe. He told the police he set fire to the building on his own initiative as a protest against the Nazis, using a few fire lighters, a rolled-up newspaper and a box of matches. It seems that van der Lubbe, who had no connection whatsoever to the German Communist Party, was in contact with SA extremists in the days leading up to the fire. Indeed, Göring later claimed that he was behind the whole escapade, but this was probably idle boasting. It is generally thought by historians that van der Lubbe acted alone.

The political significance of the Reichstag fire is more important than who started it. Hitler used the fire as a convenient excuse to arrest all Communist

Göring the Butcher. This 1933 photomontage by the anti-Nazi, John Heartfield, alleges Nazi involvement in the Reichstag fire. (Hermann Göring was Minister of the Interior at this time, organising the political police force which was later incorporated into the Gestapo. He was made head of the Luftwaffe, the German air-force, in 1935.)

Party leaders and introduce a virtual state of martial law. He decided not to ban the Communist Party immediately, in case their votes switched to the Social Democrats in the forthcoming election. On 28 February 1933, the day after the fire, Hitler issued a decree for the 'protection of the people and state'. This wide-ranging set of emergency powers allowed him to suspend all individual and civil liberties, assume complete control of the individual state governments and place all political opponents in 'protective custody'. This emergency decree – announced as a 'temporary measure' – stayed in force during the whole period of Nazi rule.

The election results, 1933

Given the remarkable events which occurred during the only democratic election under Hitler's rule, it is surprising the Nazis did not win a landslide victory. The NSDAP gained 43.9 per cent of the vote (17.2 million votes) and won 288 seats. The Catholic Centre Party increased its vote from 4.2 million in November 1932 to 4.4 million votes. The Social Democrats lost 70,000 votes, but remained the second largest party. The Communist Party ended up with 4.8 million votes – a loss of 1 million. But considering that all Communist leaders were in jail, it was a highly respectable result. The German National People's Party, Hitler's coalition partners, polled 3.1 million – an increase of 200,000 voters since the previous election. The Nazi Party, with the support of the 52 seats held by the German National People's Party, held an overall majority in the Reichstag of just 16 seats.

The Enabling Act, 1933

Of course, the main aim of the election was to give Hitler enough votes in the Reichstag to put an end to parliamentary democracy. The device Hitler used to create a one-party dictatorship was called the Law for the Alleviation and Distress of People and Reich (the Enabling Act). On 23 March 1933, the members of the Reichstag, except those in the Communist Party, who were not allowed to take their seats, were asked to turn over all legislative power to Hitler. The venue for the demise of German democracy was the Kroll Opera House in Berlin. Only the Social Democrats had the courage to vote against the Enabling Act, which passed with 441 for and 84 against. Hitler told the Social Democrats present: 'The star of Germany is in the ascendant, yours is about to disappear, your death-knell has sounded.'[2] The passing of the Enabling Act freed Hitler from any legal restraint from the Reichstag, the President and the voters. It was a significant move on the road towards dictatorship.

The legal revolution

The Nazis enacted a 'legal revolution' during 1933. The process towards Nazi domination over Germany was called *Gleichschaltung* (co-ordination), a process designed to bring the nation under total Nazi political control. On 2 May 1933, the trade unions were banned, their leaders arrested and their funds and assets confiscated. It was the turn of the political parties next. The Communists had already been banned during the election campaign. On 19 June 1933, the Social Democratic Party was voluntarily dissolved. The next party to disappear was the German National People's Party. This was wound up on 29 June. On 4 July, the Catholic Bavarian People's Party disbanded. The following day, the Catholic Centre Party was dissolved. On 14 July 1933, the NSDAP was the only political party left. By the end of July 1933, Hitler was the leader of a one-party state and every member of the Reichstag was a Nazi. The press was also swiftly brought under Nazi domination.

The problem of the Nazi radicals

The Nazi revolution from above completely destroyed democracy, the free press, the trade unions and all political parties, but the power of big business, the President, the old aristocracy and the army remained intact. Even within the Nazi Party itself there was a group of radicals with strong anti-capitalist views. The most prominent radical was Ernst Röhm, leader of the storm troopers, who numbered over 2 million street fighters. Röhm wanted an ill-defined 'Second Revolution', during which the SA, the *Schutzstaffel* (SS – Hitler's personal protection squad) and the army would be merged into a new 'People's Army'. The radical Nazis also called for the introduction of socially radical policies, including curbs on monopolies and the nationalisation of land.

These calls by Nazi radicals for a 'Second Revolution' made big business and, especially, the army officer class extremely anxious. Hitler had always expressed doubts about the anti-capitalist strand of Nazi Party ideology. He saw the SA as a group of street fighters, not the backbone of a modern army. In July 1933, Hitler told the radicals in the Nazi Party: 'The stream of revolution must be guided into the safe channel of evolution.' To calm the fears of big business, Hitler said 'ability' should guide appointments in big business, which would remain 'free of party interference'.[3] To ease the worries of the army further, Hitler told the SA leadership that: 'The Reichswehr [army] is the sole bearer of arms in the state.'[4] These reassurances to the army and big business caused great disillusionment among the Nazi mass movement.

The Night of the Long Knives, 1934

By the summer of 1934, the army leadership, supported by Hindenburg, put pressure on Hitler to sacrifice the SA or face the prospect of losing power. Even within the Nazi Party, Röhm was becoming dangerously isolated. Göring, in charge of the Gestapo (Geheime Staatspolizei), the Nazi secret police force, and Himmler, chief of the SS, both favoured a blood purge of the SA. The seriousness of the situation was brought home to Hitler on 21 June 1934, when he was invited to meet Hindenburg, by now old and frail, and General von Blomberg, the War Minister, at Neudeck. Hitler was given a virtual ultimatum by the President: either deal strongly with the SA or the army would take power. Hitler acted swiftly and decisively. On 30 June 1934 (the Night of the Long Knives), Röhm, all the major leaders of the SA and many of Hitler's other major opponents were killed in cold blood. The precise number killed was never fully established, but the figure of 401 appears accurate. Many of those killed were old enemies of Hitler, such as the 'socialist' Nazi Gregor Strasser and General von Schleicher, the last Chancellor of the Weimar Republic.

Hindenburg congratulated Hitler on his 'determined and gallant intervention'. The army leadership viewed the slaughter as necessary for 'the defence of the state'.[5] But what the army leadership did not fully appreciate was that while the blood purge had destroyed the political influence of the SA, it had increased the power and influence of the SS, which now became a major rival to the army officer class within the hierarchy of the Nazi state.

The death of Hindenburg

On 2 August 1934, President Hindenburg died. Hitler became President and added the title of Führer (leader) of the German nation. Hitler also used Hindenburg's death to force the army to swear an oath of personal allegiance to him as Supreme Commander of the Armed Forces and head of the German state. On 19 August 1934, 90 per cent of German voters (38 million) gave their approval to Hitler becoming an absolute dictator, with a mere 10 per cent voting against (4.25 million). At the triumphant Nuremberg rally of September 1934, Hitler proclaimed in front of thousands of Nazi supporters: 'There will be no other revolution in Germany for a thousand years!'[6]

Hitler strides in triumph through massed ranks of troops to speak at a rally at Bückeberg in 1934.

The Nazi state

The state which emerged from these remarkable events was a right-wing dictatorship, led by a single dominant leader (*Führer*), with an official state ideology (Nazism) and one single political party (the NSDAP). The German constitution under Nazi rule became 'the will of the Führer', carried out by a Nazi elite of ministers, free of any political restraints from parliament, the press or pressure groups. Nazi Germany was a personal dictatorship – not a one-party state. Hitler was paramount, the fountain source of all power – not the Nazi Party. It would be wrong, however, to suggest that Hitler's rule was based exclusively on terror, force and intimidation. Hitler always believed popular support was a vital factor in enhancing the authority of a personal dictator.[7] He was a very popular leader and his popularity grew throughout the 1930s.

The Führer

At the top of the Nazi political system was the Führer (Adolf Hitler), who had, in theory at least, unlimited state power. Hitler saw the Nazi state as an instrument of his own unlimited power over the Nazi Party and the German nation. Orders were given by the Führer and followed without discussion. The key to power and influence in Nazi Germany was having access to and support from Hitler. In reality, Hitler could not control or decide on every issue.[8] In spite of his claims about government in Nazi Germany being one omnipotent will, decision making was channelled through a Nazi elite and a multiplicity of conflicting and overlapping organisations.[9]

The leadership style of Adolf Hitler

One of the most important ways of understanding the complex nature of the Nazi state is to examine the eccentric leadership style of Adolf Hitler. The Nazi dictator did not live up to his carefully manipulated propaganda image as a strong and efficient leader. The centre of German government was in Berlin, in northern Germany. But Hitler spent more time at his purpose-built mountain retreat at Berchtesgaden (the Berghof), in southern Germany. He often conducted the government of Nazi Germany comfortably seated in an armchair in his own living room. He disliked bureaucratic procedures, paperwork, meetings and administration.

Hitler was an extremely eccentric administrator of a modern state. A day in the life of the Führer would often follow a pattern. He would stay in bed until after 11.00 a.m., then he read the newspapers before a leisurely late breakfast. He would only begin meeting government and party advisers at midday. There were times when Hitler would sign extremely important policy documents without giving them a second glance. Those Nazi ministers who knew his routine well would go to the Berghof and attempt to charm Hitler in order to get his agreement to a particular line of policy. For the rest of the time, ministers were expected to carry out 'the Führer's will', which was, of course, open to wide interpretation. This led to considerable variation in the way policies were implemented.

Lunch at the Berghof would not begin until 2 p.m. and often continued, usually with ministers and party officials present, until 4.00 p.m. Hitler would then go off for a short walk, his only exercise of the day, with his favourite Alsatian dog (Blondi) and an SS guard. When he returned, there would be coffee and usually chocolate cake. This was followed by a nap, or reading a book (usually on history or astrology). There would be dinner at 9 p.m. with another group of Adolf's acolytes. This was nearly always followed by a viewing of the latest German or a Hollywood film in Hitler's purpose-built projection room. After the film was over, Hitler would return to his favourite armchair in the living room and give a long (and very boring) monologue (usually about 'the old days' in Munich), which could go on well into the early hours of the next morning. The Nazi dictator would usually not go to bed until 3 a.m. and because he suffered from insomnia would often take sleeping tablets.

Hitler constantly talked about the great benefits of physical fitness, but he led a very unhealthy lifestyle. He did not smoke or drink and was a vegetarian (he actually claimed in future everyone would become a vegetarian!), but he was not healthy. He took very little exercise, played no sport and suffered from a number of painful stomach disorders, including gallstones, stomach cramps, heartburn and ulcers. He was something of a hypochondriac: the type of person who always fears any pain is the onset of a life-threatening illness. He took all manner of vitamin supplements and drugs, administered by his own personal physician, the eccentric Dr Morell, who, for a long time, even gave Hitler tablets made from the excrement of a Bulgarian peasant – in order to cure his stomach disorders. During the war years, Hitler became more or less a junkie, taking all manner of pep pills and pain-killing injections to keep going.

In spite of his eccentric lifestyle, his dislike of administration and his increasing dependence on drugs, it would be wrong to depict Hitler as the weakest link in the Nazi political system. Disputes in Nazi Germany were not about Hitler's power, which was undisputed, but concerned disagreements and power struggles among subordinates, about who was most loyally carrying out the Führer's will. These disputes strengthened Hitler's own position because they allowed him to 'divide and rule', by playing off one group against another. Hitler was not greatly interested in social or economic policy and generally allowed others to take the initiative in those areas, but on foreign policy and military preparations Hitler did play a decisive role in all the major policy decisions.

The dual state

In the early years, Nazi Germany was really a 'dual state', consisting of representatives from the old conservative establishment and a new leadership group drawn from the Nazi Party. It was a situation in which traditional groups sought to preserve independence and power, while activists in the Nazi governing group demanded greater party control in all spheres of society. This tension and conflict went on throughout the period 1933–45, with the Nazi elite gradually getting the upper hand. The dual functions of traditional state and party organisations inevitably led to conflicts of interests and greatly reduced administrative efficiency.

Central government

Hitler retained the traditional practice in central government of having individual government departments led by single ministers in charge of different areas of interest. Each government department was run as a distinct area of individual power by the minister in charge, who formulated policy and presented it to Hitler for approval. Most of the leading Nazi figures (Goebbels, Göring, Himmler, Hess, Bormann, Ley, Speer and Ribbentrop) created their own empires for personal gain and profit.

Until the late 1930s, however, three key ministries remained under the control of non-Nazi members of the 'old guard': von Blomberg (War Minister), von Neurath (Foreign Minister) and Dr Schacht (Economic Minister). It was only after February 1938 that every government ministry was under the control of a member of the Nazi elite. It is only after this date that the power structure of the dual state shifted more markedly towards the Nazi Party.

As a collective group, the cabinet did not co-ordinate policy or discuss major policy decisions. Hitler had no interest in calling cabinet meetings, preferring instead to deal with each cabinet minister separately. Cabinet government gradually disappeared in Nazi Germany. In 1933, as Hitler consolidated his rule, there were 72 cabinet meetings, but by 1936 this had dwindled to six, in 1938 the cabinet met once and it never met on a formal basis ever again.

The only two requirements for a law to be passed in Nazi Germany were the agreement and the signature of Hitler. The major legislative role in passing laws did not reside with the Reichstag, or the cabinet, but was devolved to the office of the Reich Chancellery, a body directly under the control of Hitler, which circulated draft legislation between ministers and ensured each minister followed certain rules before laws were given approval. The Reich Chancellery acted as the chief administrative and legislative office of the Führer and was the major power broker between each minister and Hitler. Some ministers wanted Hitler to enact laws immediately, without even circulating their contents to other ministers. As a result, an informal system of 'Führer edicts' emerged, whereby a minister simply gained Hitler's signature for a law without even bothering to let other ministers know about it until after the event. In 1941, a Party Chancellery under Martin Bormann was established, which acted as a rival organisation to the Reich Chancellery.

To add to the confusion, Hitler frequently by-passed formal government departments to set up rival institutions and specialist agencies. It has been estimated that there were 42 separate agencies with executive power to implement policy within the central government machine of Nazi Germany. Hitler was quite aware of this confusion, but he consistently blocked initiatives designed to make the governmental structure more efficient and co-ordinated. In essence, the political system in Nazi Germany was a complex maze of personal rivalries and overlapping party and state institutions, which resulted in chaos and confusion. Nazi Germany certainly was a departure from the previously well-oiled German government machine. The failure by the Nazi state to co-ordinate policy and relate objectives to available resources was a very important factor in the ultimate collapse of the regime.

Local government

The tension between the state and the party was equally acute in local government. When Hitler took office, Germany had a federal system of government, with each individual regional government (*Land*) enjoying a great deal of autonomy to enact legislation. This system was dramatically altered by the Nazi regime. On 7 April 1933, individual German states were brought under central direction. Hitler created the new post of Reich governor (*Gauleiter*) to act as the representative of central government in each *Gau* (which replaced the *Land*). Every *Gauleiter*, usually a Nazi Party figure, directly appointed by the Nazi leader, had wide-ranging powers to carry out the Führer's policies at the local level. But Hitler confused matters by retaining the post of Minister-President for each region, who was responsible for local administration. The absence of clear lines of demarcation between the roles of the *Gauleiter* and the Minister-President led to frequent conflicts. These were not resolved by the Law for the Reconstruction of the Reich (1934), which abolished all local assemblies in the federal states and subordinated both the Reich governors and the Minister-Presidents to control of the Reich government. Local government in Nazi Germany was a two-headed monster, with both heads taking orders from and carrying out the wishes of the Führer. At the city level, the Nazis retained the post of lord mayor, but in January 1935 added the additional post of 'Delegate of the NSDAP in the Municipality' (a party official given power to appoint and dismiss the mayor and local councillors). This added yet another layer of rivalry and conflict at the local level.

The role of the party

A key reason for the confusion in the Nazi state was the incomplete revolution of 1933. Nazi Germany was a one-party state, but the party ruled in a coalition of power with old elites. It was never made fully clear in legal terms whether the party was superior or subordinate to the state at national or regional level. The exact role the party played in society was also confusing. Hitler defined the role of the party as to 'support the government in every way'. The party held all the seats in the Reichstag, but this body met only 12 times from 1933 to 1939, giving consent to four laws, and was more a rubber stamp of Hitler's views and had no legislative or debating role.

In practice, the chief role for the Nazi Party was to indoctrinate German society with Nazi ideas.[10] There was a genuine contempt among many Nazi Party activists towards the continuing power and influence of the old guard at national and regional level. The dynamism of the Nazi Party was largely used to ensure Nazi policies were carried out at the regional level. Party activists also played a leading role in organising propaganda and popular displays of public support for the regime and supporting the activities of Nazi organisations such as the Hitler Youth and the Labour Front.

Another major priority for the party was to increase its membership. This drive was extremely successful, but whether new recruits joined out of conviction or expediency is difficult to estimate. In the late 1930s approximately 25 per cent of the adult population (8 million) were members of the Nazi Party. Being a party member became important in nearly every occupation. The dramatic increase in membership became a source of tension within the party between the old 'hard core', pre-1933 Nazi members and the new recruits, many of whom were suspected of joining to improve their job prospects. The dilution of the Nazi Party after 1933 by a flood of new recruits makes it very difficult to calculate whether the aims of the true radicals coincided with the ambitions of many of the new recruits who sought to champion radical policies in order to stress their loyalty to the Führer and prosper within the Nazi state.

The economy in Nazi Germany

Adolf Hitler took office in 1933 with no clear economic ideas. The economic points in the party programme made promises to curb the monopoly powers of big business, abolish department stores (to help small traders), put limits on finance capital and give aid to small businessmen, artisans and farmers. But Hitler was luke warm towards the anti-capitalist aspects of the party programme. During 1932, he attempted to calm the fears of business leaders by telling them they had nothing to fear from a Nazi government.

Once in power, the Nazis had to develop a viable economic policy. Many leading Nazis were attracted to the ideas put forward by a group of economists who advocated a 'third way' between a fully planned socialist economy and a completely free capitalist economy. This new economic model stressed greater political direction of the economy by government to meet the needs of the state. It implied a mixture of capitalist free enterprise and state-sponsored spending on public works to reduce unemployment. A more radical idea, also supported by many in the Nazi elite (including Hitler), was the concept of autarchy (economic self-sufficiency). Under this plan, Germany would cut itself off completely from the international trading system and government would direct industry and agriculture to bring about self-sufficiency in supplies of food and raw materials. A third economic idea, also under discussion within the Nazi elite, was the concept of *Wehrwirtschaft* (war economy), which implied the organisation of the entire economy towards the needs of a future war. All these ideas formed a part of Nazi economic thinking, but they were never co-ordinated into a single economic strategy. As a result, the Nazi regime frequently pursued a number of different, often contradictory, economic policies at the same time.

The influence of Schacht, 1933–37

The most important figure in the development of Nazi economic policy from 1933 to 1937 was Dr Hjalmar Schacht, a leading conservative, well respected in business circles. He was appointed by Hitler as President of the Reichsbank in 1933 and assumed the role of Economic Minister in 1934. Schacht's financial wizardry greatly aided German rearmament. He came up with the idea of printing secret government bonds (mefo bills), which were used by the regime to place orders with industry for arms.

In September 1934, Schacht produced a 'New Plan', which froze all interest payments on foreign debts and created a system of regulating imports according to the political needs of the regime. The 'New Plan' set priorities over imports and enabled Germany to negotiate bilateral trade agreements. These agreements allowed Nazi Germany to move the bulk of its trade to Europe and to import more of its raw materials from the Balkans and South American states. In addition, there was a major shift from consumer to military production. In 1935, 25 per cent of the German economy produced consumer goods, but in 1937 the proportion of consumer goods produced shrank to 17 per cent.

At the Nuremberg trials, Schacht claimed he tried to oppose the idea of gearing the entire German economy to the needs of war and he claimed his resignation as Economic Minister on 26 November 1937 was due to a realisation that Hitler was determined to direct the German economy towards the needs of war, no matter what the economic consequences were. Of course, this was Schacht's justification for his actions. It seems he wanted a slow build-up of arms in preparation for a lengthy war, rather than Hitler's desire for a speedy build-up, which actually encouraged economic problems and helped make short wars of plunder a logical consequence of the general direction of German economic priorities.

An economic miracle? The fall in unemployment

In spite of underlying economic difficulties caused by swift rearmament, there was a major economic recovery in Nazi Germany.[11] The most impressive aspect of this recovery was a sharp fall in unemployment, from 6 million in 1933 to less than 1 million in 1938. This was hailed as an economic miracle at the time. Yet the recovery in the German economy was due to state-aided job-creation schemes, public works programmes and increased arms spending. Tax relief was given to companies to take on extra workers; autobahns were built, which were unnecessary at the time, given the very low level of car ownership, and a good deal of spending went on lavish public buildings. It is now generally recognised by economic experts that the use of public money to create jobs artificially brings no long-term economic benefits and can actually produce long-term economic problems, most notably inflation.

Economic growth in Nazi Germany from 1933 to 1938 was primarily due to the rapid growth in arms spending, not improved economic efficiency, increased exports or a major expansion in the German consumer goods industry. Even the low inflation rate Germany enjoyed in the Nazi period was created by the artificial government device of a wage and price freeze. This kept inflation much lower than it would otherwise have been in a free-market system. The claims of a Nazi 'economic miracle' can now be seen as largely a propaganda myth.

The Four Year Plan, 1936

By the summer of 1936, the 'New Plan' had not solved Germany's continued need for imports of raw materials to aid rearmament. There was a raw materials crisis, which became acute because the cost of vital imports was increasing at a time when Germany's reserves of gold and foreign currency, vital to purchase raw materials from abroad, were running out. This was the background to the most significant Nazi intervention into the field of economic policy: the Four Year Plan, introduced in September 1936.

The Four Year Plan, under the leadership of Göring (who knew nothing about economics – much less about planning), was set up alongside the 'New Plan' and made Schacht believe (quite rightly) that his position as Economic Minister was being severely undermined. The chief aim of the Four Year Plan was to make Germany self-sufficient in food and raw materials, and ready for war by 1940. Under the plan, imports were to be reduced and industries which attempted to produce synthetic rubber, oil, petrol and textiles were given increased state support. In addition, farmers were offered incentives to increase food production. From 1936 to 1940, projects linked to the Four Year Plan accounted for 50 per cent of all industrial investment in the German economy.

But the Four Year Plan did not produce economic self-sufficiency, nor prepare the German economy for war. In 1939, Nazi Germany was still importing 20 per cent of its food needs and 33 per cent of raw materials. In some areas vital to the rearmament, the need for imports was quite staggering. In 1939, Germany imported 66 per cent of its oil, 70 per cent of its copper, 85 per cent of its rubber and most of its aluminium. The manufacture of synthetic products, which required enormous government spending on research and development, did not produce immediate benefits. The German economy was not close to collapse in 1939, but it was not in a healthy condition either. The trend towards self-sufficiency and rapid arms build-up, which accelerated greatly from 1936 to 1939, was leading to great pressure to solve the problem of imports through short wars of plunder, primarily because Germany lacked sufficient foreign currency and gold reserves to purchase vital imports.

It is now generally accepted by historians that Germany never did reach the goal of *Wehrwirtschaft* in peacetime. Hitler was never prepared to allow a major cut in German living standards, which was essential for a total mobilisation of the economy for war. He wanted to spend enormous sums on rearmament and also protect the living standards of the average German family. In spite of the enormous amount of spending on armaments from 1933 to 1939, the German economy was not fully prepared for a lengthy war. Only in 1943 was the German economy brought under central planning and control to meet the needs of total war.

Big business

The big winners from Nazi economic policy were large industrial companies, especially those geared to rearmament.[12] The co-operation of big business was vital to economic recovery and for rearmament. The trend in the German economy after 1933 was towards larger companies which enjoyed a monopoly over different areas of production. In 1933, 40 per cent of German industrial production was under monopoly control, but by 1937 monopolies controlled over 70 per cent of all production.

The power of the directors of big businesses was left untouched by the Nazi regime, while the rights of shareholders were greatly curtailed. The regime directed business to support its economic and foreign policy objectives, but left the control of companies in private hands. The profits of heavy industry increased from 2 per cent of turnover in the boom year of 1928 to 6.5 per cent in 1938. For many companies, especially those involved in the rearmament programme (motor transport, fuel companies, the aircraft industry, producers of machine tools, chemicals, tanks and cars), profits rose to astronomical levels. One enormous beneficiary of Nazi rule was the giant chemical monopoly I. G. Farben, which was heavily involved in the development of synthetic goods and chemical products. Between 1933 and 1939, its profits shot up by a whopping 150 per cent and its workforce grew by 50 per cent. The managers of major industrial companies awarded themselves more perks and saw their wages rise by 50 per cent from 1933 to 1939, much higher than any other group in German society.

Small business

The much-heralded Nazi 'new dawn' for small businesses did not come to pass. One of the key promises made by the Nazis in opposition had been to close down department stores. Under the terms of the Law for the Protection of the Retail Trade (1933), department stores were prevented from providing certain services, including hairdressing, baking, shoe repairing and catering, but they were not closed down, only prevented from engaging in further expansion. Indeed, the turnover of the five leading department store chains grew by 10 per cent between 1936 and 1939. The ability to set up a new small business was greatly curtailed. In 1937, it was decreed that no individual could set up in business with capital of less than the equivalent of $200,000 and any company with capital of under $40,000 was forced out of business. This measure effectively closed down 20 per cent of all small enterprises.

Artisans, another key group of Nazi supporters before 1933, did win some important concessions. Under the terms of the Law for the Provisional Construction of German Craft Trades (1933), anyone wishing to set up in business had to hold a master qualification in a registered trade. This measure greatly aided qualified tradesmen and improved efficiency in the trade sector of the economy. Many independent tradesmen also benefited from increased spending on public buildings and from the 500-mark subsidy given to home owners to install toilets and bathrooms. In spite of these measures, the number of independent artisans declined from 1.65 million to 1.5 million between 1936 and 1939.

The farmers

Another group expecting to benefit greatly from Nazi rule were farmers.[13] As we have already seen, Nazi electoral support before 1933 was strongest in rural areas. In Nazi propaganda, the farmer was hailed as a hero. Given this, the Nazi regime had to offer some land reform to satisfy rural Germany. The economic position of those who worked on the land did improve somewhat under Nazi rule. From 1933 to 1937, agricultural prices increased by 20 per cent and the wages of agricultural labourers increased faster than those in industry.

The most significant agricultural reform introduced by the Nazi regime was the Hereditary Farm Law (1933), which ensured all farms up to 308 acres became the hereditary estates of the families who owned them and could not be sold, mortgaged or closed owing to debts. Only an 'Aryan German citizen' who could prove 'purity of blood' dating back to 1800 was allowed to own a farm. The Hereditary Law fulfilled a long-held desire of peasants to remain on the land they owned, but the clause preventing them from selling their land bound farmers to the soil in a way not seen since feudal times, and the clause preventing them mortgaging their property made it difficult for hard-pressed farmers to raise loans to improve efficiency. The major beneficiaries of the Hereditary Farm Law were the existing owners of large estates and commercial farms. A total of 18 per cent of all land was owned by the richest 0.5 per cent of farmers, while 66 per cent of land was owned by farmers with estates between 12 and 250 acres. Only

18 per cent of farmers owned less than 12 acres of land and most of these lacked modern equipment and even a piped water supply.

Industrial workers

One group who did not expect to benefit from Nazi rule were industrial workers, the majority of whom had not supported the Nazi Party before 1933. All trade union rights were removed. Unions were replaced by a Nazi substitute organisation called the Labour Front (*Deutsche Arbeitsfront*; DAF), led by Robert Ley, which aimed to 'create a true social and productive community'.[14] Nazi employment laws did away with contracts of employment and defined the employer as 'master' and the employee as 'follower'. The radical leaders of the Nazi Factory Cell Organisation (NSBO) were purged and the NSBO was forced to accept the domination of the Labour Front. Ley claimed that the NSBO had been set up by Gregor Strasser with similar aims to the trade unions and because it ignored the wishes of the employers it was now incompatible with National Socialist ideology.[15]

In theory, the Labour Front was supposed to be an honest broker between the interests of the employers and labour. In practice, it was a vital means of controlling employees, ensuring they did not make demands for increased wages. The Labour Front ensured the employer was 'the leader' of the factory, while the worker was expected to further the aims of the employer. In the workplace, wages were set and imposed by Labour Front trustees, who nearly always followed the wishes of the employer.

The Labour Front made cosmetic efforts to improve the leisure activities of the workers. A very important organisation set up for this purpose was called *Kraft durch Freude* ('Strength through Joy'), which encouraged employers to provide workers with sport and fitness facilities. The Labour Front also provided extremely cheap holidays for workers. It seems most workers took advantage of many of the leisure benefits offered by the Labour Front, but remained largely indifferent to Nazi propaganda about the Labour Front being for the benefit of workers.

The economic position of workers was not greatly improved by the Nazi regime. In many cases, the overall position was much worse. Hourly wages for skilled workers fell by 1 per cent and for unskilled workers by 3 per cent between 1932 and 1939. Some skilled workers, especially those involved in industries connected to rearmament, were better off. In addition, the introduction of 'performance-related pay' served to benefit a few individuals. In general, however, the take-home pay of industrial workers fell further because of increases in income tax and health insurance deductions. The number of hours worked per week by each worker increased by 15.2 per cent from 1932 to 1939. The average industrial worker in Nazi Germany in 1936 was putting in 47.8 hours per week, a figure which was nearly eight hours more than the average British industrial worker. Higher wages were achieved only by working longer hours. These long hours may help to explain why fatal accidents at work in Nazi Germany increased dramatically, from 217 in 1932 to 525 in 1936. The mobility of workers was also greatly restricted. Each employee was required to carry a workbook listing skills and experience, but the employer had the right to retain the workbook of any employee, or blacklist a worker from gaining employment elsewhere.

The standard of living in Nazi Germany

Perhaps the most persistent myth about the Nazi regime was that it greatly increased the standard of living for the German people. There was certainly a 'feel good factor' in Nazi Germany, stoked up by Nazi propaganda. The great majority of German people felt better off than they had in the depths of the depression. There were some economic improvements from the years of depression. From 1932 to 1938, the amount of food consumed in Germany increased by 18 per cent, clothing sales went up by 25 per cent and sales of furniture and household goods rose by 50 per cent.

Economic experts agree that the greater the proportion of income spent by a person on food, then the lower is that person's overall standard of living. In 1938,

Hitler opening a Volkswagen (people's car) factory in May 1938. Hundreds of thousands of Germans took part in a government savings scheme, putting aside five marks per week, to purchase their own Volkswagen. The factory, however, was converted to make military vehicles and people were cheated of their savings as the small number of 'Beetles' produced were allocated to SS officers and other Nazi elites.

the average German spent 45 per cent of income on food (compared with 41 per cent in Britain). The average German consumed four times as much bread as the average American. Beef consumption in Nazi Germany (a good indicator of affluence in the 1930s) between 1933 and 1938 was 33 per cent below the US level. In 1938, Germans purchased 25 per cent less butter than the British, ate 50 per cent fewer eggs and purchased 50 per cent less sugar. Only in the consumption of milk and cheese did the German level match the British level. The average German ate 50 per cent more potatoes (the cheapest vegetable) than the average British person and alcohol consumption grew faster in Nazi Germany than in Britain between 1933 and 1939. Beer sales were at a very similar level to Britain during the Nazi era, but wine, brandy and champagne sales were higher, which tends to suggest the rich grew richer under the Nazi regime. Tobacco consumption in Germany also went up by 50 per cent. Increased consumption of alcohol and tobacco suggests an increase in underlying stress and tension in Nazi society.

The demand for consumer goods increased, but whether Nazi Germany was a consumer society is less clear. The greatest symbol of consumer affluence in the 1930s was the ownership of a car. In 1936, German car ownership stood at 500,000, compared with 1 million in Britain and 23 million in the USA. By and large, the German people under Nazi rule had a lower standard of living than people in Britain and were vastly worse off than people in the USA. What the Nazis did achieve in their economic policy, largely through successful propaganda, was to get Germans to think they were much better off than they actually were.

The Nazi state and economy

2.1 Hitler's power as dictator: the view of a Nazi constitutional expert

The position of Führer combines in itself all sovereign power in the Reich; all public power in the State as in the movement is derived from the Führer power. If we wish to define political power . . . we must not speak of 'State Power' but of 'Führer Power'. For it is not the State as an impersonal entity which is the source of political power, but rather political power is given to the Führer as the executor of the nation's common will. Führer power is comprehensive and total; it unites within itself all means of creative political activity; it embraces all aspects of political life; it includes all national comrades who are bound to the Führer in loyalty and obedience. Führer power is not restricted by safeguards and controls, by autonomous protected spheres, and by vested individual rights, but rather it is free and independent, exclusive and unlimited.

Source: Ernst Rudolf Huber, *Verfassungsrecht des Grossdeutschen Reiches*, Hamburg, 1939, p. 142

2.2 Hitler's style of leadership: the view of Hitler's press chief

In the twelve years of his rule in Germany Hitler produced the biggest confusion in
government that has ever existed in a civilized state. During his period of government,
he removed from the organization of the state all clarity of leadership and produced a
completely opaque network of competencies. It was not laziness or an excessive degree
of tolerance which led the otherwise so energetic and forceful Hitler to tolerate this real
witch's cauldron of struggle for position and conflicts over competence. It was
intentional. With this technique he systematically disorganized the upper echelons of
the Reich leadership in order to develop and further the authority of his own will until it
became a despotic tyranny.

Source: Otto Dietrich, *Hitler*, London, 1955, pp. 127–32

2.3 Hitler's style of work: the view of a member of Hitler's personal staff

He disliked the study of documents. I have sometimes secured decisions from him,
even ones about important matters, without his ever asking to see the relevant files. He
took the view that many things sorted themselves out on their own if one did not
interfere. And he was by no means wrong about that . . . One still sometimes hears the
view that Hitler would have done the right thing if people surrounding him had not kept
him wrongly informed. Hitler refused to let himself be informed. Unfortunately, that
was not only the case in domestic affairs but in foreign affairs as well . . . How can one
tell someone the truth who immediately gets angry when the facts do not suit him?

Source: Fritz Wiedemann, *Der Mann, der Feldherr werden wollte*, Ketwigg, Germany, 1965,
pp. 69–70, 77, 90

2.4 Hitler on the role of the Nazi Party, 1934

The Führer stressed:

The most essential tasks of the Party were:
1. To make the people receptive for the measures intended by the Government.
2. To help carry out the measures which have been ordered by the Government in the
nation at large.
3. To support the government in every way.

Furthermore, the Führer stressed that those people who maintained that the revolution
was not finished were fools; they did this only with the intention of getting particular
jobs for themselves. The Führer described what difficulty he had in filling all the posts
with the right people and went on to say that we had people in the movement whose
conception of revolution was a permanent state of chaos . . . The Party must bring about
the stability on which Germany's future depended. It must secure this stability.

Source: J. Noakes and G. Pridham, *Nazism 1919–1945. A documentary reader, Vol. 2: State,
economy and society*, Exeter, 1984

2.5 Hitler on Germany's economic situation, 1936

We are overpopulated and cannot feed ourselves from our own resources . . . we lack foodstuffs and raw materials; what matters is the taking of those measures which can bring about a final solution for the future and a temporary easing of conditions during the transition period . . . The final solution lies in extending our living space, that is to say, extending the source of raw materials and foodstuffs of our people. It is the task of the political leadership to one day solve this problem . . . The temporary easing of conditions can be achieved only within the framework of our present economy . . . There can be no building up of raw materials for the event of war just as there can be no building up of foreign exchange reserves. The attempt is sometimes made today to represent matters as if Germany went to war in 1914 with well-prepared stocks of raw material. That is a lie. No country can assemble in advance the quantities necessary for war lasting longer than, say, one year. But if any nation were really in a position to assemble those quantities of raw materials needed for a year, then its military, political and economic leaders would deserve to be hanged . . . There is only one interest, the interest of the nation; only one view, the bringing of Germany to the point of political and economic self sufficiency . . . In short, I consider it necessary that now, with iron determination, a 100 per cent self sufficiency should be attained in every sphere where it is feasible and that not only should the national requirements in these most essential raw materials be made independent of other countries, but we should also thus save the foreign exchange which in peacetime we need for our imports of food stuffs.
I, therefore, set the following tasks:
1. The German armed force must be operational within four years.
2. The German economy must be fit for war within four years.
Source: *Documents on German foreign policy*, series C, Vol. v, No. 490, London, 1949–82

2.6 German exports and imports, 1933–39 (in millions of marks)

Year	Imports	Exports	Balance
1933	4,204	4,871	+667
1934	4,451	4,167	−284
1935	4,156	4,270	+114
1936	4,218	4,768	+550
1937	5,468	5,911	+443
1938	5,449	5,257	−192

Source: J. Noakes and G. Pridham, *Documents on Nazism*, London, 1974, p. 417

2.7 Dr Schacht on the relationship between rearmament and the standard of living

Reduced to a simple formula, the problem is as follows: The credit money made available for armament purposes produces a demand for consumers' goods through the payment of wages and salaries. The armament manufacturers, however, deliver military goods which are produced but not put on the market. From this follows two consequences: first, care must be taken that aside from armament manufacture sufficient consumer goods are produced to sustain the population including all those working in the armaments industry; second, the less there is consumed, the more the labour can be used for armaments; but the higher consumption rises, the more the manpower must be left for consumer goods. Therefore, the standard of living and the extent of armament production are in an inverse ratio.

Source: J. Noakes and G. Pridham, *Documents on Nazism*, London, 1974, p. 392

Document case-study questions

1 Identify the main features of Hitler's constitutional position as Führer as outlined in 2.1.

2 What impressions of Hitler's leadership style can be gained from 2.2?

3 What does 2.3 tell us about Hitler's attitude towards administration?

4 What conclusions about Hitler's view of the role of the party in the Nazi state can be drawn from 2.4?

5 Evaluate briefly the significance of Hitler's views on the economic situation in 2.5.

6 What conclusion can be drawn from the statistics on German trade outlined in 2.6?

7 What insights does 2.7 provide into the economic policies of the Nazi regime?

Notes and references

1 K. Hildebrand, *The Third Reich*, London, 1984, p. 3.
2 A. Bullock, *Hitler. A study of tyranny*, London, 1962, p. 270.
3 W. Shirer, *The rise and fall of the Third Reich*, London, 1960, p. 257.
4 J. Toland, *Adolf Hitler*, London, 1976, p. 450.
5 Shirer, *Third Reich*, p. 281.
6 *Ibid.*, p. 287.
7 D. Smith, *The left and right in twentieth century Europe*, London, 1970, p. 59.
8 See E. N. Peterson, *The limits of Hitler's power*, Princeton, 1969.
9 For a detailed discussion see M. Broszat, *The Hitler state*, London, 1981.
10 See J. Noakes (ed.), *Government, party and people in Nazi Germany*, Exeter, 1980.
11 For a full evaluation of the German economy see R. Overy, *The Nazi economic recovery 1932–1938*, London, 1982.
12 See A. Schweitzer, *Big business in the Third Reich*, London, 1964.
13 See J. E. Farquharson, *The plough and the swastika*, London, 1976.
14 See R. Smelser, *Robert Ley: Hitler's Labour Front leader*, London, 1988.
15 J. Noakes and G. Pridham, *Nazism 1919–1945. A documentary reader, Vol. 2: State, economy and society*, Exeter, 1984, p. 337.

3 Life inside Nazi Germany: social and cultural developments

Evaluating the impact of Nazi rule on German society is extremely difficult. Some historians view Hitler's rule as 'revolutionary', while others see it as 'counter-revolutionary'. Nazi propaganda made grandiose claims about Hitler being determined to create a *Volksgemeinschaft*, which would put an end to rigid class divisions and privileges, thereby transforming Germany into a truly classless society. Yet Hitler had no grand plans for social reform. The social and cultural policies of the Nazi regime were primarily concerned with moulding the attitudes of the German people towards supporting its aims.

The rituals of Nazi power

The Nazi swastika symbol was on every flag, uniform and building. A series of new Nazi bank holidays to mark events such as Hitler's birthday (20 April), the Nuremberg rally of the Nazi Party (September) and to mourn those Nazis killed in the failed Munich beer hall putsch (November) were also introduced. Hitler worship was a national pastime. Photographs of Hitler were pinned up everywhere. Every newly married couple was given a free copy of *Mein Kampf* to take on their honeymoon. There was even a legal obligation on every German (except in the army until 1944) to greet every other person by raising a hand skyward and shouting 'Heil Hitler'. The projection of Hitler as a demi-god seems to have worked. Hitler was viewed as a popular figure by the vast majority of the population.

One of the most high-profile Nazi social events was a vast annual charity collection – known as Winter Relief. Every winter, especially around Christmas, leading Nazis could be seen standing underneath giant Christmas trees in German towns and cities holding giant buckets into which passing Germans were expected to put money. A giant scoreboard was placed in Berlin's city centre, which gave a running total of all the money raised. Winter Relief raised millions of marks each year, which was used to give a food hamper to old-age pensioners.[1]

Property ownership

A close examination of property ownership in Nazi Germany shows there was little alteration to the existing distribution of wealth. Private industry was not taken into the ownership of the state. Junker landowners retained their vast estates, even though the aristocracy was not restored to its pre-1914 power-political position. A sixth of all arable land was owned by a mere 17,070 Junker families, representing 0.5 per cent of all farmers. The major confiscation of property in Nazi Germany was from the Jewish community. Most Jewish land and property found its way into the hands of a disparate selection of pro-Nazi leaders, activists and small businessmen in a completely ad hoc fashion.[2]

The army

There was little sign of a social revolution within the German army. In 1939, for example, 11 field marshals, the highest army rank, came from the old aristocratic Junker class, while the remaining seven were of upper-middle-class origin. Most social mobility within the officer class was at the rank of general, where the aristocratic element was reduced from 61 per cent to 25 per cent between 1920 and 1936. The German army resisted Nazi Party penetration until the latter stages of the Second World War. From 1933 to 1938, the army is best described as an independent collaborator with Hitler as German leader which was able to place itself above party politics.

By and large, the older generation of officers in the army were not Nazis. They are more accurately described as old-style German nationalists. But among younger officers there was a growing enthusiasm for Nazism. There was an undeniable tension between the army leadership and the SS leadership during the Second World War. Even so, the overall attitude of the army was generally positive towards the military aims of the regime, up until the moment when the campaign against the Soviet Union started to falter.[3] The key turning point in the weakening of the power of the army within the state was the failed bomb attempt on Hitler's life on 20 July 1944 (see Chapter 4). Only after this event did Hitler decide to undertake a purge of the old aristocratic element at the top of the army. Indeed, Hitler blamed his military defeat on his failure to enact a social revolution within the higher ranks of the army.

Law and order

The Nazi Party was more successful in gaining control over the agencies of law and order. The dominant Nazi security forces were the black-shirted SS and the Gestapo.[4] The SS – led by Heinrich Himmler – began life in the 1920s as the elite bodyguard of Hitler. During the mid-1930s the SS gained control over the entire German uniformed police and then over the activities of the Gestapo. A closely related security service to the SS was the SD (*Sicherheitsdienst* – state security service) led by the young and ambitious Reinhard Heydrich.

The SS played a crucial role in establishing and staffing Nazi concentration camps in Germany where the 'domestic enemies of the state' (Marxists, liberals, Freemasons and renegade Christians), along with Nazi 'racial enemies'(Jews and Gypsies) and 'moral enemies' (habitual criminals, gays, prostitutes and vagrants) were imprisoned. The chief role of the Gestapo was to find out information about 'enemies of the state'. It used to be thought that Nazi Germany was a vast police state, but recent research has shown that the SS, SD and the Gestapo were greatly helped in tracking down 'enemies of the state' by ordinary German people who acted as informers within the local community.

The changes which the Nazis made to the criminal justice system made it difficult for any group or individual to contemplate opposing the regime. The civil liberties each citizen had enjoyed under the Weimar constitution vanished. Judges were appointed on the understanding they always acted in the interests of the National Socialist state. Lawyers were required to become members of the Nazi Lawyers' Association. The role of the defence council, crucial to a fair trial, was greatly weakened. State prosecutors were advised to punish the individual criminal in any way they saw fit rather than establishing a uniform system of penalties for each crime. As a result, there was a wide variation in the penalties imposed for similar crimes in different parts of Germany.

The extremely repressive nature of Nazi justice is most graphically illustrated by reference to the greatly increased use of the death penalty. In 1932, only three crimes carried the death penalty, but between 1933 and 1945 a total of 46 carried it. It was very rare for any criminal to avoid a lengthy prison sentence. A more alarming trend was the Nazi practice of not releasing prisoners at the end of their sentences, but instead moving them to concentration camps. The Nazi regime's harsh sentencing structure did produce a substantial fall in criminal offences – from 590,165 in 1933 to 335,162 in 1939.

The incidence of murder, house burglary, theft and mugging all declined significantly. All beggars – defined as 'anti-socials' – were cleared from the streets, often ending up in concentration camps. On the other hand, prosecutions for rape and illegal abortion increased by 50 per cent and for homosexuality (due to the systematic Nazi persecution of gays) by a staggering 900 per cent. Oddly enough, the number of burglaries, especially from food shops and railway freight trucks, increased steeply. The criminal justice system was also used to persecute Jews and political opponents of the regime.

The harshest treatment by the Nazi regime before 1939 was reserved for political prisoners, especially Communists and socialists. The Gestapo had the right to take anyone into 'protective custody' without the need for a trial. Former members of the Communist Party suffered greatly from this law, with 300,000 Communists being arrested and put in concentration camps. Of these, 30,000 were executed. The Nazi crackdown on crime was popular with a great majority of the German people – especially among the suburban middle classes, who saw it as a sign of a return to stability. Nazi propaganda stressed that 'political opponents', 'law breakers', 'deviants' and 'anti-social elements' had to be treated harshly for the national community to prosper.

The family

At the centre of Nazi society was 'the family'. A famous Nazi slogan called the family 'the germ cell of the nation'. The Nazi regime did make a great effort to increase the popularity of marriage and increase the birth-rate. The advertisement of contraceptives was banned, but not their sale. All birth-control clinics were closed down. The number of children born outside marriage declined from an average of 150,000 per year in 1932 to 100,000 per year by 1939. In the same period, the birth-rate in Nazi Germany among married couples increased substantially. In 1914, the German birth-rate was 33 per 1,000 of the population; by 1932 it had fallen alarmingly to 14.7 per 1,000.

The Nazi regime used special welfare benefits to increase the popularity of marriage and motherhood. Newly married couples were offered a 1,000-mark loan, repayable at 3 per cent interest, which was reduced by 25 per cent after the birth of each child. This meant a couple could turn their marriage loan into an outright free gift by producing four 'healthy' children. From 1933 to 1938, a total of 1,121,000 marriage loans were paid out, but 980,000 of these were cancelled due to births. In 1938, a family allowance of 10 marks per month was introduced for the third and fourth child of a marriage and a 20-mark additional allowance for every subsequent child. By 1939, the birth-rate had shot up to 20.4 per 1,000, an increase of 39 per cent since 1932. But it remains a matter of dispute as to whether the increased birth-rate was a direct result of Nazi welfare policies aimed at the family, or was due to the optimism which accompanied economic recovery.[5]

To increase the popularity of family life further, the Nazi regime attempted to raise the status of mothers. A famous Nazi poster depicted a mother holding a baby under the slogan 'I have donated a child to the Führer'. The mother who stayed at home to bring up children was depicted as a national hero in Nazi propaganda. On 12 August (the birthday of Hitler's late mother), every mother who had given birth to a large number of children was awarded a Mother's Cross (gold for eight children, silver for six and over, bronze for four and over). Hitler claimed that a prolific mother had the same honoured place in society as a front-line soldier. But not just anyone was allowed to have children. The Law for the Prevention of Hereditary Disease (1933) imposed compulsory sterilisation on any male or female suffering from mental retardation or handicap, physical disability, epilepsy, blindness, deafness or venereal disease. By 1937, 102,218 men and 95,165 women had been sterilised under this legislation.[6]

Education

Schools

Another key aim of the Nazi regime was to indoctrinate the young with a new set of ideas. The most obvious way to do this was through the existing education system. Hitler gave the job of Reich Minister of Science, Education and Popular Culture to Bernhard Rust, an ex-schoolmaster who had been sacked in 1930 because of 'mental instability'. In keeping with Nazi ideology, Rust forced German schools to downgrade intellectual skills and upgrade the importance of practical skills and physical fitness. The number of sport and fitness lessons increased from two to five one-hour periods, at the expense of religious lessons. New textbooks were produced to fit in with Nazi ideology. History and biology were given increased emphasis. All schools added a history course on the rise of the Nazi Party, while biology lessons concentrated on Nazi ideas on race and heredity. The teaching of science, chemistry and mathematics greatly deteriorated.

The teaching profession was brought under Nazi control. All teachers were subjected to political vetting. Those found 'politically or racially unsuitable' were dismissed. In addition, all teachers were enrolled in the Nazi Teachers' Association. The general anti-intellectual emphasis in German schools, which Nazi educational policies encouraged, led to a distinct loss of status for teachers, followed by a severe teacher shortage in many subjects. Between 1932 and 1938, the number of qualified elementary teachers fell by 17,000. The Nazi regime dealt with this teacher shortage by lowering qualification standards. Party membership increasingly ranked more highly in the selection of new teachers than formal teaching qualifications.[7]

The universities

The German universities, world leaders in so many subjects, went into a sharp decline under the Nazi regime. Hitler had utter contempt for professors and the academic life of universities. After 1933, the independence of the universities was severely restricted. Rectors, deans and leaders of student unions were appointed by the Nazi state. The Association of University Lecturers became a Nazi lap dog. Between 1933 and 1939, a total of 2,800 lecturers and over 300 full professors were dismissed for political and racial reasons. But the great majority remained in post and did not oppose the brutal destruction of a significant body of German intellectual and scientific knowledge.

The teaching of a new subject, 'The Racial Sciences', which focused on Hitler's crude racial theories, became a very fashionable subject, while the teaching of the natural sciences went into a steep decline. Many brilliant scientists, most notably Einstein and Frank in physics, fled abroad. They were followed by many other world experts in chemistry and mathematics. The downgrading of the value of a university education by the Nazi regime led to a dramatic fall in the number of university students, from 127,920 in 1933 to 58,325 in 1938. All university students were obliged to undertake four months of labour service in an SA camp and to engage in three hours of sport per week as part of their degree studies. The Nazi regime tended to emphasise that there was a sharp difference between the sheltered and privileged world of academia and the harsh reality of real life.

Youth

The Nazi Party created a rival organisation to the formal education system – the Hitler Youth (*Hitler-Jugend*) – which indoctrinated the young with Nazi ideas. The expansion of the Hitler Youth, under the leadership of Baldur von Schirach, the son of a German aristocrat, was quite remarkable. In 1932, the Hitler Youth had 100,000 members, by 1936 there were 6 million members, and by 1939 approximately 90 per cent of German youth were members. The failure to achieve 100 per cent membership of the organisation was due to the difficulties poor families encountered in paying for uniforms, monthly subscriptions and the costs of staying at summer camps.

The Hitler Youth drilled young Germans to accept Nazi concepts of race, discipline and obedience. Its chief slogans were 'Youth must be led by youth' and 'We are born to die for Germany'. The Hitler Youth organised summer camps at which political indoctrination, physical fitness, rifle practice, endurance and team-building games were core activities. Its success in indoctrinating young people with Nazi ideas and improving physical fitness appears to have been limited. The continual emphasis on obedience grew tiring for many members. Many parents reported that their children frequently returned home from Hitler Youth camps injured and very often exhausted.[8]

The grand claims made in Nazi propaganda about service in the Hitler Youth transforming the health of the young are not borne out by statistics. From 1933 to 1937, diphtheria, scarlet fever and infantile paralysis doubled. In 1936, one in three 18-year-old conscripts to the German army suffered from flat feet. More alarmingly, the juvenile share of crime went up by 300 per cent between 1933 and 1939.

The German Girls' League, the female equivalent of the Hitler Youth, encouraged girls to improve their physical fitness, but it concentrated mostly on developing the domestic skills required of a future wife and mother. Whenever boys from the Hitler Youth and the German Girls' League got together, sex was very high on the agenda. In 1936, for example, when members of the Girls' League and the Hitler Youth attended the Nuremberg rally together, over 900 girls returned home pregnant. It seems membership of the Hitler Youth or German Girls' League did not break traditional patterns of friendship among the young, who continued to draw their closest friends from the school and the local neighbourhood.

Women

Women in Nazi Germany could be in no doubt they lived in a male-dominated world. The Nazi regime very strongly opposed ideas of equality and equal rights for women (although they did retain the vote). The feminist movement of the Weimar period was projected by Nazi propaganda as led by 'trouser-wearing' and 'man-hating' women. The Nazi movement insisted that women and men had distinctly different roles in life. Goebbels claimed that the main tasks of women were to 'be beautiful', to bring 'children into the world' and only take jobs 'suitable for a woman'.

In Nazi Germany, women were expected to be wives and mothers, while the men wore the uniforms, the jackboots and, especially, the trousers. The Nazi regime deprived women of the right to be judges or local or national political representatives. There was talk of all married women being forced to give up their jobs. But economic reality forced a climb-down. Female labour, especially in unskilled jobs, was very cheap. Between 1933 and 1939, the number of women in employment increased from 5 million to 7.4 million. At the start of the war, women were not called up for either military or labour service. Only in 1943 were women finally conscripted to work for the war effort.

The Nazi Party created three women's organisations – the German Women's Enterprise, the National Socialist Womanhood and the Reich Mothers' Service – to indoctrinate women with Nazi ideals. The major activity of the German Women's Enterprise, which boasted 5.8 million members, was 'consumer advice', placing great emphasis on encouraging women to attend cookery courses. The National Socialist Womanhood had 2.8 million members and aimed to promote 'the nation's love life, marriage, motherhood, the family, blood and race, youth and nationhood'. The Reich Mothers' Service predominantly promoted child care. By March 1939, over 1.7 million German women had attended one of its organised courses. These Nazi women's organisations did not have a major impact, except in so far as they reinforced the male-dominated Nazi view of women's role in society.[9]

Propaganda

Another important place in which the Nazi regime wanted a revolution was in the heads of the German people. The Nazi regime created a Ministry of Propaganda and Popular Enlightenment, under Joseph Goebbels (the original

Joseph Goebbels addressing a meeting in the Congress Hall, Nuremberg, 1935. Goebbels was a brilliant speaker and his radio broadcasts reached into every German home. After Hitler's death, Goebbels and his wife poisoned their six young children and then committed suicide in Hitler's bunker in 1945.

'spin doctor'), to unite the nation behind the aims of the regime.[10]
A number of separate Reich 'chambers' were set up to regulate and control
literature, the press, music, the fine arts, the theatre, radio and films. These
often competed with the Propaganda Ministry for control over the minds of the
German people.

The press

The Nazis imposed total control over the mass media, which in the pre-television
age was dominated by the press, radio and the cinema. Germany had a
predominantly regional press. In 1933, there were 4,700 regional newspapers,
but only 2.4 per cent of them supported the Nazi Party. By 1944 there were fewer
than 1,000 regional newspapers and 82 per cent swore 'total allegiance' to the
Nazis, with the remainder 'loyal' to the regime. On coming to power, the Nazi
regime closed down all socialist and Communist newspapers. All newspaper
editors and journalists were forced to pledge an oath of allegiance to the regime.
Germany had only one major national newspaper – the *Völkischer Beobachter*,
the Nazi Party newspaper, which increased its circulation from 116,000 in 1932 to
1,192,000 in 1941. Every day, the editors of the Berlin daily newspapers and
representatives of the regional press were given a briefing by the Propaganda
Ministry on what news they could and could not print, what pictures they should
use and what comments they should write. In this way, the same Nazi arguments
featured in every German newspaper, locally and nationally.

Radio

The Nazis saw radio as another very important area of propaganda. Radio, the
leading form of home entertainment, was confined to one single outlet, the Reich
Broadcasting Corporation, which was firmly under Nazi control. In 1933, 4.5
million households owned a radio, but by 1942 16 million German households
had one (70 per cent of all households). Hitler often used radio to communicate
directly with the German people. In 1933 he gave over 50 radio broadcasts.
Indeed, Hitler's last public speech, in July 1944, was on radio. The Nazi regime
used radio not so much for political indoctrination but to give orders to the
population. In between Nazi diatribes was an endless diet of light entertainment
and classical music, which accounted for 70 per cent of all radio broadcasts.

Cinema

The Nazi regime also used the cinema for propaganda purposes. The newsreels
were used to announce important political and social developments. All the films
we now see of Adolf Hitler are the carefully crafted work of the Ministry of
Propaganda, which projected the Nazi leader as a demi-god leading wildly
enthusiastic crowds. The remainder of cinema output consisted of feature films,
nearly all of which were love stories, comedies, crime thrillers and musicals.
Goebbels viewed the cinema as a form of escapism and avoided using feature
films as outright vehicles of Nazi propaganda. Even so, every film script was
vetted by the Propaganda Minister before it went into production. As with other

branches of the arts, a great deal of cinema talent fled abroad, most notably the director Fritz Lang, and Marlene Dietrich and Peter Lorre, who both became Hollywood stars. Going to the cinema was an extremely popular pastime in Nazi Germany and attendance grew by 400 per cent between 1933 and 1942.

Literature

The most potent example of the Nazi attitude towards literature was the ceremonial book burnings which took place in 1933. Thrown onto the flames of Nazi hate were books by Europe's greatest writers, scientists and thinkers, including Thomas Mann, Albert Einstein, H. G. Wells, Karl Marx and Emile Zola. Works by over 20,000 other writers were banned. Many noted contemporary German writers fled into exile. Those writers who remained turned out books which they knew the regime would approve of. In place of the anti-war and pacifist literature of the Weimar period came a stream of pro-war and militaristic eulogies that portrayed German troops in the trenches of the First World War as a band of patriotic and united brothers robbed of victory by socialists and Communists at home. The setting for a great deal of Nazi fiction was the rural community. Indeed, the impression given in most Nazi literature is not of an advanced industrial society but of a predominantly farming community. Even this dreary diet of politically prejudiced literature did not put Germans off reading books. Sales of books increased and the number of state-run libraries grew from 6,000 in 1933 to 25,000 in 1940. The most widely bought book in Nazi Germany was, of course, *Mein Kampf*, which sold over 6 million copies.

The theatre

The theatre was also purged of everything the Nazis disliked. Works by many of the great German playwrights, most notably Bertolt Brecht, Ernst Toller and Georg Kaiser, were banned. Most leading Jewish writers, directors and actors took their talent overseas. In their place, the Nazis produced a wide range of political plays and musicals. Political plays proved a great turn-off to most theatregoers, who remained predominantly educated and middle class. To placate the needs of the existing audience there was a revival of classical plays, including those of Shakespeare and Schiller. Oddly enough, plays by the left-wing Irish writer George Bernard Shaw were performed in Nazi Germany, apparently because Hitler liked the way Shaw poked fun at the English class system.

Music

Classical music, the least political of the arts, was subject to the least Nazi censorship. Of course, works by Jewish composers – such as Mendelssohn and Mahler – were banned, along with many of the experimental composers of the Weimar period. The most famous living composer in Germany, Richard Strauss, did not leave; he was appointed President of the Reich Chamber of Music. The Berlin Philharmonic Orchestra retained its brilliant level of performance and operas by Wagner – Hitler's favourite composer – enjoyed enormous popularity.

The fine arts

The art world suffered very badly from the Nazi drive towards conformity. Over 6,500 major works by modern artists were removed from display in museums and art galleries. Hitler branded modern art as 'degenerate', and claimed: 'Anyone who sees and paints a sky green and pastures blue ought to be sterilised.' In place of modern art came 'Aryan art', which focused on the portrayal of physical and military power, female beauty and idyllic rural life.

Hitler was most passionately interested in architecture. He wanted his regime to leave a lasting impression through its great civic buildings. He sponsored huge and enormously costly architectural projects. Nazi architecture was in the grand classical style, emphasising the pomp and power of Nazi rule. 'The greater demands the state makes of the people,' Hitler commented in 1937, 'the more imposing it must look to them.'

Health

Another way in which the Nazis claimed they wanted to create a revolution was in the physical health of the German people. In the beginning, the Nazis inherited a highly developed health service. The regime increased the number of doctors by 19,000 from 1933 to 1943, but this was achieved at the cost of reducing the training period for doctors from five to three years. There was a quite alarming fall in the number of medical specialists, from 16,500 to 9,500, between 1938 and 1944. A total of 5,500 highly trained Jewish doctors were banned from practising during the late 1930s, which did further harm to the overall condition of the German health service.

There were obviously some benefits to the health of the nation under the Nazi regime. The system of medical screening for all newly weds and for those applying for family allowances helped in the early detection of some diseases, especially tuberculosis. Increased sporting facilities in factories helped improve the physical fitness of workers. For example, 5 million Germans held the 'Strength through Joy' fitness certificate. The infant mortality rate went down from 77 per 1,000 births in 1932 to 60 by 1939 (the British level was lower, at 53 per 1,000).

But the overall health of German people deteriorated under Nazi rule. Alcoholism and smoking increased rapidly. More alarming was the very steep rise in the suicide rate, from 18,934 in 1932 to 22,288 in 1939 (double the British level) and there was also a very large increase in the number of fatal accidents, from 28,870 in 1932 to 39,767 in 1939. There were an average of 8,000 people killed in road accidents every year from 1933 to 1939 (compared with 6,000 per year in Britain, where car ownership was twice as high). Death from industrial accidents went up by 33 per cent under the Nazi regime.

The number of people admitted to hospital increased from 4 million in 1932 to 5.8 million in 1938. Local doctors in Nazi Germany reported a very high incidence of absenteeism from work due to stomach disorders, which tends to suggest a high degree of underlying stress within the working population.

Dentists also reported very poor dental health of the population. In 1937, a study of 350 families of industrial workers showed that over 25 per cent had no toothpaste. Cancer and tuberculosis were below the British level, but between 1933 and 1939 diphtheria doubled, heart disease rose and scarlet fever, typhoid and polio were all at much higher levels than in Britain during the 1930s.

It should also be emphasised that, as an economy, surgery was usually performed in Germany during the 1930s without anaesthetic, which resulted in more operative and post-operative deaths than in Britain and the USA, where anaesthetic was in general use. The decline of scientific and chemical research in German universities may help to explain why there were fewer major medical advances in Nazi Germany. There were far fewer X-ray facilities in Nazi Germany than were available in Britain during the 1930s. By and large, the health of the people of Nazi Germany compares very unfavourably with democratic Britain and the USA from 1933 to 1945. It shows that Nazi claims about creating a healthy 'master race' were very much a propaganda myth.[11]

Document case study
Life inside Nazi Germany

3.1 Joseph Goebbels on the role of propaganda, March 1933

It is not enough for people to be more or less reconciled to our regime, to be persuaded to adopt a neutral attitude towards us, rather we want to work on people until they have capitulated to us, until they grasp ideologically that what is happening in Germany today not only must be accepted but also can be accepted. Propaganda is not an end in itself, but a means to an end. If the means achieves the end then the means is good . . . The aim of our movement was to mobilise people, to organise people, to win them for the national revolutionary ideal. This aim – even the most hostile person cannot dispute this – has been achieved and that represents the verdict on our propaganda methods. The new Ministry has no other aim than to unite the nation behind the ideals of the national revolution.

Source: J. Noakes and G. Pridham (eds.), *Nazism 1919–1945. A documentary reader, Vol. 2: State, economy and society*, Exeter, 1984, p. 381

3.2 Joseph Goebbels defines the relationship between the Nazi regime and the press, March 1933

The press is not only there to inform but must also instruct. In saying this, I am directing my remarks above all to the national press. You will also recognise that it is an ideal situation for the press to be a tremendously important instrument for influencing the masses, which in the hands of the Government can be used in the areas for which it is responsible. It is possible for the Government and the press to cooperate with one another on the basis of mutual trust. I regard it as one of the principal tasks to achieve that. I am aware of the significance of the press. I recognise what it means to have a good or a bad press. I regard myself, therefore, so to speak as the senior link man between government and press. I will make sure that contact is never interrupted. For this reason I see in the task of the press conference to be held here daily something other than what has been going on up to now. You will of course be receiving information here, but also instructions. You are to know not only what is happening but also the Government's view of it and how you can convey that to the people most effectively.

Source: J. Noakes and G. Pridham (eds.), *Nazism 1919–1945. A documentary reader, Vol. 2: State, economy and society*, Exeter, 1984, p. 393

3.3 An American reporter reports on a Nazi book-burning ceremony, May 1933

The whole civilised world was shocked when on the evening of 10 May 1933 the books of authors displeasing to the Nazis . . . were solemnly burned on the immense Franz Josef Platz between the University of Berlin and the State Opera on Unter den Linden. I was a witness to the scene. All afternoon Nazi raiding parties had gone into public and private libraries, throwing on to the streets such books as Dr Goebbels in his supreme wisdom had decided were unfit for Nazi Germany. From the streets Nazi columns of beer hall fighters had picked up these discarded volumes and taken them to the square above referred to. Here the heap grew higher and higher, and every few minutes another howling mob arrived, adding more books to the impressive pyre. Then, as night fell, students from the university, mobilised by the little doctor [Goebbels], performed veritable Indian dances and incantations as the flames began to soar skyward.

Source: Louis Lochner (ed.), *The Goebbels diaries 1942–43*, Washington, DC, 1948, pp. 177–80

3.4 The memories of a Hitler Youth leader

What I liked about the HJ [Hitler Youth] was the comradeship. I was full of enthusiasm when I joined the Jungvolk at the age of ten. What boy isn't fired with high ideals such as comradeship, loyalty and honour. I can still remember how deeply moved I was when we learned the cub mottoes: 'Jungvolk boys are hard, they can keep a secret, they are loyal; Jungvolk boys are comrades; the highest value for a Jungvolk boy is honour.' And then the trips! Is there anything nicer than enjoying the splendours of the homeland in the company of one's comrades . . . In addition, I was pleased that sport also had its place in the Jungvolk. We never went on our trips without a ball or some other piece of sports equipment. Later, however, when I became a leader in the Jungvolk the negative aspects became obvious. I found the compulsion and the requirement of absolute obedience unpleasant. I appreciated that there must be order and discipline in such a large group of boys, but it was exaggerated. It was preferred that people should not have a will of their own and should totally subordinate themselves. But this approach could not educate the boys into becoming strong willed men.

Source: A. Klonne, *Jugend im Dritten Reich. Die Hitler-Jugend und ihre Gegner*, Düsseldorf, 1980, p. 80

3.5 Nazi instructions to schools on the teaching of history, 1938

The teaching of history must bring the past alive for the young German in such a way that it enables him to understand the present, makes him feel the responsibility of every individual for the nation as a whole and gives him encouragement for his own political activity . . . The course of history must not appear to our young people as a chronicle which strings events together indiscriminately, but, as in a play, only the important events, those which have a major impact on life, should be portrayed in history lessons. It is not only the successful figures who are important and have an impact on life, but also the tragic figures and periods, not only the victories, but also the defeats. But it must always show greatness because in greatness, even when it intimidates, the eternal law is visible.

Source: J. Noakes and G. Pridham (eds.), *Nazism 1919–1945. A documentary reader, Vol. 2: State, economy and society*, Exeter, 1984, p. 438

3.6 Hitler on the role of women, 1934

The slogan 'Emancipation of Women' was invented by Jewish intellectuals and its content was formed of the same spirit . . . If the man's world is said to be the state, his struggle, his readiness to devote his powers to the service of the community, then it may perhaps be said that the woman's world is a smaller world. For her world is her husband, her family, her children and her home. But what would become of the greater world if there was no one to tend and care for the smaller one? How could the greater world survive if there were no one to make the cares of the smaller world the content of their lives? No, the greater world is built on the foundation of the smaller world. Providence has entrusted to the woman the cares of that world which is her very own, and only on the basis of this smaller world can the man's world be formed and built up. The two worlds are not antagonistic. They complement each other, they belong together, just as man and woman belong together.

Source: *Frankfurter Zeitung*, 9 September 1934

3.7 The basic principles of the National Socialist Womanhood, 1933

1. We desire the awakening, the training, and the renewal of women's role as the preserve of the nation's springs: the nation's love life, marriage, motherhood and the family, blood and race, youth and nationhood. The whole education, training, careers and position of women within the nation and state must be organised in terms of their physical and mental tasks as mothers.

2. We recognise the great transformation which has taken place in women's lives over the past fifty years as a necessity produced by the machine age, and approve of the education of women for the good of the nation in so far as they are not performing their most immediate service for society in the form of marriage, the family and motherhood.

3. We regret, however, the false paths of the democratic–liberal–international women's movement because it has not found new paths for the female soul rooted in GOD, and his nation . . .

4. We desire a women's movement of renewal which reawakens those deepest sources of female strength and strengthens women for their particular tasks in the freedom movement and in the future Germany.

5. We demand and therefore carry out the fight against the planned denigration and destruction of women's honour and women's dignity and against the moral corruption of youth.

6. We erect against it the will of German women which is rooted in GOD, nature, the family, the nation and fatherland.

Source: D. Klinksiek, *Die Frau im NS-Staat*, Stuttgart, 1982

Document case-study questions

1 What does 3.1 tell us about Goebbels' attitude towards propaganda?

2 In the light of Goebbels' comments in 3.2, outline what you believe was the role of the press in Nazi Germany?

3 Comment on Lochner's reaction in 3.3 to the book-burning ceremony in 1933.

4 Offer an evaluation of the views expressed on the Hitler Youth in 3.4.

5 What light does 3.5 shed on the teaching of history in German schools under the Nazi regime?

6 Offer an evaluation of Hitler's view of the role of women in Nazi Germany as outlined in 3.6.

7 What role does the National Socialist Womanhood assign to women in Nazi society in 3.7?

Notes and references

1 R. Grunberger, *A social history of the Third Reich*, London, 1971, pp. 101–22.

2 D. Geary, *Hitler and Nazism*, London, 1993, p. 48.

3 See J. Noakes and G. Pridham (eds.), *Nazism 1919–1945. A documentary reader, Vol. 3: Foreign policy, war and racial extermination*, Exeter, 1988, pp. 624–47.

4 For a detailed analysis see J. Delarue, *The history of the Gestapo*, London, 1964.

5 Noakes and Pridham, *Nazism, Vol. 3*, pp. 448–70.

6 *Ibid.*, p. 458.

7 Grunberger, *Third Reich*, pp. 362–85.

8 Noakes and Pridham, *Nazism, Vol. 3*, pp. 416–47.

9 Grunberger, *Third Reich*, pp. 320–39.

10 See E. K. Bramstead, *Joseph Goebbels and National Socialist propaganda 1925–1945*, London, 1965.

11 Grunberger, *Third Reich*, pp. 282–97.

4 Opposition and resistance inside Nazi Germany

Nazi propaganda gives the impression that the regime was very popular, while opposition and dissent carried the probability of arrest, imprisonment and even execution. Nevertheless, most historians do accept there was a large measure of consent and popular support for Hitler's regime, and that opposition and resistance lacked popular support. It was, in Kershaw's phrase, 'Resistance without the People'.[1]

The actual level of opposition and resistance to Hitler is very difficult to calculate.[2] 'Resistance' can be defined broadly to embrace every type of action or behaviour which showed open opposition to the regime, or it can be narrowly defined as actions taken by individuals who attempted to overthrow it. Many historians use the term 'opposition' to encompass all acts of public defiance, but reserve the term 'resistance' to the small group of individuals who were willing to risk their lives to overthrow the Nazi state by force. If we accept these definitions, we can see the opponents of Nazi rule were a larger group than the active resisters.[3] The aim of this chapter is to identify groups and individuals inside Nazi Germany who attempted to oppose and resist Hitler's regime.

The church

The Christian churches (Protestant and Catholic) expressed opposition to the attempt by the Nazis to undermine long-standing Christian doctrines and practices. The Christian churches were the only organisations in German society allowed to retain complete organisational autonomy. Germany was divided religiously by the Reformation into the Protestant north and the Catholic south. Hitler frequently attacked the churches for 'ignoring the racial problem'. In the long term, Nazism and Christianity were incompatible. After all, the Nazis were educating the German people to see Nazism as the 'national religion'.

The Protestants of Germany numbered 45 million and belonged to various Lutheran and reformed churches. The Nazis wanted a centralised and unified Protestant church. In July 1933, the 28 provincial Protestant churches were amalgamated into a single Reich Church, under the leadership of Bishop Ludwig Müller. The aim of the Nazi Party was to use a group called the 'German Christians' (dubbed the 'SA of the Church') to promote Nazi ideas within the church. This drive towards Nazification provoked a reaction from a dissident group calling itself the 'Confessional Church', led by Reverend Martin Niemöller, who was alarmed by the Nazi desire to remove the Old Testament (dubbed by

Nazis as a 'Jewish book') from worship. The Confessional Church saw itself as the legitimate custodian of Protestantism. This brave stand led to a crackdown within the Reich Church. Members of the Confessional Church were bullied, beaten and arrested by the Gestapo.

The church struggle caused Hitler great embarrassment. In July 1937, Niemöller was placed in 'protective custody', which he remained under until 1945. In addition, 800 pastors of the Confessional Church were also put in concentration camps. To defuse the row, Hitler decided to return control of the Protestant church to the official church establishment in return for a promise that it would offer no further resistance to the regime. At the same time, Hitler dropped his attempt to control the church through the German Christians and their influence declined. The struggle by the Protestant church to retain religious autonomy was strengthened by the backing of millions of churchgoers.

The Catholic church was more united in organisation and outlook than the Protestant church. The allegiance of German Catholics to Roman Catholicism survived the Reformation. In July 1933, Hitler signed a concordat with the Vatican promising to guarantee the freedom of the Catholic Church to regulate its own affairs on condition it withdrew from politics. Not long afterwards, the Nazi regime was undermining the concordat by establishing groups within the Catholic Church to disseminate Nazi propaganda, by suppressing the activities of Catholic schools and youth organisations and by banning Catholic newspapers. These developments made the leadership of the Catholic church very disillusioned. There was a strong fight by the Catholic church to retain its own organisations and schools, a struggle that was eventually lost. Another struggle by the Catholic church, to retain the use of the crucifix in Catholic churches, was successful. The strength of Catholic opposition to the regime is emphasised by the fact that a total of 400 Catholic priests were incarcerated in the Dachau concentration camp alone. By and large, the Catholic church avoided open confrontation in case this provoked further intimidation. It seems Catholic non-conformity towards the regime did find substantial support in many Catholic regions and attendances at Catholic churches in Nazi Germany increased substantially, especially during the Second World War.[4]

The army and Foreign Office

There were strong elements of resistance within the army and among other conservative elites within the Nazi state. The army was another area of German society which retained some degree of autonomy from the Nazi Party.[5]

The Beck–Goerdeler Group

A group at the forefront of army resistance to the Nazi regime was the Beck–Goerdeler Group. This group was led by two conservative figures: Colonel Ludwig Beck, a leading army figure, and Carl Goerdeler, the Lord Mayor of Leipzig. Beck was chief of the army general staff from 1935 to 1938. The first attempt by the army to overthrow the Nazi regime was planned by Beck during the Czech crisis of 1938. Beck was worried that Hitler would engineer a war over Czechoslovakia and he was determined to organise a coup to prevent this. To this end, he sent emissaries to Britain to warn the British government of Hitler's aggressive designs against Czechoslovakia, but the conspiracy failed to get off the ground because Beck received no encouragement whatsoever from Neville Chamberlain, the British Prime Minister. Utterly dismayed, Beck resigned from his post, after the signing of the Munich agreement, and became a key figure in a complex network of conspirators who were determined to overthrow the Nazi regime. Beck was the most influential figure within the resistance.

Closely associated with Beck was Dr Carl Friedrich Goerdeler, who resigned as Mayor of Leipzig in 1937, outraged by a Nazi order to remove a statue of the Jewish composer Mendelssohn from the town centre. Goerdeler, a devout Protestant and monarchist, was the leading civilian figure within the elite resistance to Hitler. He worked closely with Beck to build up a network of opponents to the Nazi regime in the Foreign Office, the army, the Berlin police and the intelligence services.[6]

The Beck–Goerdeler Group wanted Hitler replaced not by a parliamentary democracy but by an authoritarian regime based on tolerance and the rule of law – a state much like pre-1914 Germany. Although they rejected the methods of the Nazis, the group did not want Germany to become a second-rank power and took it for granted that a post-war German government would dominate central Europe.

The Foreign Office

Closely linked with the Beck–Goerdeler Group were opponents of the Nazi regime at the Foreign Office. The Foreign Office never became a fully fledged Nazi organisation. A number of Foreign Office diplomats worked closely with the resistance, most notably Adam von Trott zu Solz, who was heavily involved in negotiations with British and US diplomatic and intelligence officials in Switzerland and Sweden over a possible diplomatic agreement with Germany in the event of Hitler being deposed.

Another leading member of the Foreign Office resistance group was Ulrich von Hassell, former German ambassador in Rome. He undertook diplomatic negotiations on behalf of the resistance movement with British intelligence sources in the latter stages of the war.[7]

Abwehr

A group linked with the resistance figures in the Foreign Office was Abwehr, a state organisation which dealt with military intelligence. Abwehr gave valuable information about Hitler's movements to the army group of conspirators and was another important means through which the resistance built up contacts with agents and diplomats overseas. Abwehr established a secret dossier on Nazi war crimes (the *Zossen* documents), which they hoped could be used in a war trial of Hitler and leading Nazis. The two leading figures within Abwehr most closely involved in the resistance to Hitler were Admiral Wilhelm Canaris, a monarchist with right-wing opinions, and Colonel Georg Hansen, a right-wing conservative.

Von Stauffenberg and the failed bomb plot of 1944

At the centre of this complex network of opposition were officers within the German army. The leading resistance figures in the army were Major-General Henning von Tresckow, a key figure in Army Group Centre, leading on the eastern front; Field Marshal Erwin von Witzleben, who was to have assumed the role of commander-in-chief of the armed forces in the event of a successful coup against Hitler; and Colonel Claus Graf Schenk von Stauffenberg, the leading figure in the attempted assassination of Hitler on 20 July 1944.

Von Stauffenberg, a devout Catholic, was born in 1907 of a south German aristocratic family. He was the great-grandson of a military hero of the Prussian army during the Napoleonic Wars. During the late 1930s he rose swiftly up the ranks of Hitler's army, but his sympathies were with the old aristocracy not with Nazism. During the Russian campaign von Stauffenberg became completely disillusioned with Hitler's rule. In 1943, he was posted to Tunisia to help the German army resist the onward march of the US army, but on 7 April 1943 his car was hit by enemy fire and he lost an eye, his right hand and two fingers of his left hand in the incident. These injuries seem to have made von Stauffenberg even more disillusioned with Hitler's war. It seems he decided to remain in the army for one reason: to kill Hitler.[8] To organise the assassination, von Stauffenberg became closely involved with the Beck–Goerdeler Group. What distinguished him from many of his co-conspirators was his desire to create a social democracy in the event of Hitler's death. He wanted to include Julius Leber, a leading social democrat, and Wilhelm Leuschner, a former trade union leader, in the first post-Nazi cabinet.

The number of army officers involved in the conspiracy to kill Hitler grew markedly during 1943. The most well-known army figure recruited by the conspirators was Field Marshal Erwin Rommel, the 'Desert Fox'. Rommel thought it might be better to arrest Hitler and put him on trial for war crimes rather than make a martyr of him by killing him. In 1943, there were no less than six attempts made by army conspirators to kill the Nazi dictator. The nearest the conspirators came to success was on 13 March 1943, when a time bomb planted on Hitler's plane on a flight from Smolensk to Rastenburg failed to go off. One problem the conspirators faced was Hitler's strong suspicion of a conspiracy against him within the army, which encouraged him to frequently change the venue and times of meetings and speeches at the last moment.

It was in the summer of 1944, with Germany heading for defeat, when the conspiracy to kill Hitler became more urgent. The leading army conspirators opened up negotiations with British and US diplomats concerning the possibility of an armistice in the event of a successful coup against Hitler. The conspirators even asked for a separate peace settlement with Britain and the USA, to allow the war with the Soviet Union to continue. These overtures were completely rejected by the western allies, who insisted there would be no separate peace.

In spite of this rebuff, the army conspirators decided to make an attempt on Hitler's life at one of the daily military meetings he held at his military headquarters at Rastenburg, east Prussia. On 20 July 1944, von Stauffenberg left a bomb in a suitcase under a table, while Hitler was chairing a meeting, and sneaked away by car to Berlin. The bomb went off as planned, but Hitler survived with only minor injuries. The coup failed and the conspirators were rounded up.

The aftermath of the 1944 bomb plot

The failed attempt on Hitler's life led to a ferocious crackdown on all opposition groups. On the evening of the failed assassination attempt, Hitler told German radio listeners a coup by a 'clique of ambitious, conscienceless, and criminal and stupid officers' had failed and would be dealt with in 'true National Socialist fashion'.[9] Von Stauffenberg was shot dead the same evening; Beck committed suicide; and von Tresckow killed himself the following day. The remaining figures involved in the plot were rounded up and put on trial. Even family members of those accused were arrested, imprisoned and, in many cases, executed. Many leading conspirators were hanged on meat hooks, suspended by piano wire. The failed bomb plot allowed the Nazis to crush the complex network of elite resistance groups. Approximately 5,000 conspirators and opponents of the regime were executed, many of whom came from leading aristocratic families.

It is quite easy to view the conservative army conspirators as the engine room of resistance to Hitler. But this view must be qualified by the knowledge that a great many of them withdrew support from Hitler only because his form of nationalism was more extreme than their own version, which was still expansionist and authoritarian. A 'moderate' Hitler, pursuing limited territorial objectives, was fine; it was the out of control Hitler they did not like.

Communist resistance

There were many other groups involved in resistance to Hitler. The largest resistance group were the Communists.[10] The Communist Party was a bitter opponent of the Nazi Party before 1933 and was ruthlessly crushed once Hitler came to office. Of the 300,000 members of the party in 1933, 150,000 were imprisoned in concentration camps and approximately 30,000 were executed (the largest death toll of members of any of Germany's pre-1933 political parties). These figures illustrate why the Communists were determined to resist the Nazis, but they also help to explain why they feared the consequences of openly challenging the regime.

Instead, the Communists set up secret underground groups who produced anti-Nazi literature, often distributed in industrial areas to factory workers. Many railway workers were involved in distributing anti-Nazi pamphlets. The Communists were also involved in daubing anti-Nazi graffiti and posters on walls in major cities and in helping to organise industrial sabotage. In 1936, for example, the Communists organised a strike at the Auto Union works in Berlin to protest against the Olympic Games.

Many Communist leaders who fled Germany in 1933 engaged in propaganda through the Communist International. Communist resistance was damaged somewhat by the Nazi–Soviet Pact of 1939, but it revived after the German attack on the Soviet Union. Most active Communists were never reconciled to the Nazi regime and looked forward to the day when it would be defeated in war. The underlying strength of the Communist Party was revealed in the first free elections held in the industrial Ruhr after 1945, when it received 20 per cent of the vote.

Red Orchestra

A subgroup of Communists, also engaged in resistance activities, was the Red Orchestra (*Rote Kapelle*). The group had influential contacts in the Air and the Economics Ministries, and passed on secret information about Nazi war plans to the Soviet Union. The members of the Red Orchestra were sympathetic to the Soviet Union. Among its disparate membership were civil servants, artists, writers, intellectuals and workers, who produced anti-Nazi pamphlets and discussed their common dislike of authoritarian rule in small underground groups. The Gestapo eventually discovered the identities of the leaders of the group, who were put on trial and executed in 1942.

The Kreisau Circle

Another very interesting group of opponents to the Nazi regime was the Kreisau Circle.[11] This was an elite dinner-party debating society which held meetings at Kreisau Castle in Silesia, the ancestral home of Count Helmut James von Moltke, the great-grandnephew of the famous field marshal. The members of the Kreisau Circle were a loose collection of people, mostly between the ages of 36 and 50, primarily drawn from the land-owning aristocracy, the civil service, the church and members of the old Social Democratic Party. The members of this small circle hated Hitler, but they never contemplated removing him by force. All they did, between 1942 and 1944, was engage in polite discussions about the type of government which should follow after Hitler's defeat in the Second World War. The group acted as a meeting place for those who desired a democratic society, based on a form of Christian socialism. The Kreisau Circle accepted that Germany would suffer territorial losses after the war, but Adam von Trott zu Solz, a leading member of the group, argued that Germany should retain the Sudetenland and parts of west Prussia in any post-war settlement. After the bomb plot against Hitler, the activities of the group were uncovered by the Gestapo. Most of the leading figures were hanged, as von Moltke claimed at his trial, 'merely for talking'.

Industrial workers

The largest group which engaged in isolated acts of defiance against the Nazi regime were industrial workers. It now seems clear that acts of worker resistance and opposition were far more common than was admitted by Nazi propaganda. There was a high level of worker resistance in big industrial cities. In Dortmund prison, for example, of the 21,823 prisoners serving time for political opposition, the vast majority recorded their occupation as 'industrial worker'. The same is true of the prison records in most other industrial regions. The reports of the Gestapo show widespread worker protest over food price rises in 1935. There were even strikes by workers building the motorways in the mid-1930s. Deliberate slow working on production lines in armament factories became such a widespread problem it was made a criminal offence in 1938. But strikes and slow working were not widespread and the vast majority of workers were controlled and neutralised by the regime. A very large number retreated into political apathy, many exhibiting a 'reluctant loyalty' towards the regime.[12]

Social Democrats

The Social Democratic Party did vote against the Enabling Act, but voluntarily disbanded shortly afterwards. The leaders of the party fled into exile, residing in Prague from 1933 to 1937 and Paris from 1937 to 1940. The Social Democrats in exile devoted a great deal of time to producing anti-Nazi pamphlets and 'SOPADE' reports, which were smuggled into Germany and distributed among workers. The SOPADE reports indicate the Nazi regime did persuade the average person 'to leave politics to the people at the top' and showed that many former supporters of the Social Democratic Party turned inward towards private life. The major problems for the Social Democrats inside Nazi Germany were a lack of finance and leadership and continued animosity from the Communists.

New Beginning

A fringe opposition group on the socialist wing of the Social Democratic Party was New Beginning (*Neu Beginnen*). It was influenced by the ideas of Lenin. The members of this small group discussed what the future of Germany should be after Hitler. New Beginning favoured a left-wing coalition government consisting of the Social Democrats, socialists and Communists. The leaders of the group saw disunity among the left as one of the key reasons why Hitler came to power in the first place. The group produced illegal pamphlets which advocated these ideas, but it failed to win over the Communist and Social Democratic Parties for its idea of a broad left coalition. As a consequence, its loosely organised followers drifted away.

University students ('White Rose Movement')

One of the most poignant attempts to protest openly against the Nazi regime was undertaken by university students in Bavaria in 1943. The focus of student discontent against Hitler was the University of Munich. The protest was led by Sophie Scholl, a biology student, and her brother Hans, a medical student. The group, known as the White Rose, produced letters and leaflets opposing Nazism and the war, which were sent to students in all universities in southern Germany. One leaflet proclaimed: 'Nothing is less worthy of a cultivated people than to allow itself to be governed by a clique of irresponsible bandits.'[13]

In February 1943, Paul Giesler, *Gauleiter* of Bavaria, gave a speech to students at the University of Munich during which he derided the male students as 'physically unfit' to fight in the war, and urged female students to give up their studies and 'produce a child a year for the Führer'. In a spontaneous act of defiance, the students howled down Giesler, ejected the SA from the hall and marched in a demonstration through Munich against the Nazis. This was the first major public demonstration against Hitler's rule seen on the streets of Germany since 1933. Sophie Scholl said that as so many people had died for the regime, it was about time some died fighting against it. The Nazi regime acted quickly to put down the White Rose Movement. Hans and Sophie Scholl were arrested, beaten up and hauled before the 'People's Court', where they were sentenced to death by guillotine.[14]

Youth protest

There were many other young people who engaged in acts of defiance against the regime. Admittedly, these groups were a minority, but they do illustrate that

The Nazi penalty for adolescent non-conformity: a group of young *Edelweisspiraten* are executed in public in Cologne, 1944.

youth was not completely brainwashed by Nazi propaganda. Sometimes youth protest was simply non-conformist behaviour, such as listening to banned American jazz and swing records. These groups became known as 'Swing Youth' and 'Jazz Youth'. They were actually monitored by the Gestapo, who often mounted raids on illegal jazz clubs. A more serious problem was the growth of street gangs in many working-class areas of major cities. Many of these gangs beat up members of the Hitler Youth. Two of the most well known of them were called the 'Raving Dudes' and the 'Navahos', names which reveal the growing influence of American culture on a certain section of German youth. Many street gangs sang American hits of the day, smashed up shops and daubed anti-Nazi graffiti on walls and public buildings. One notable example of street gang graffiti, daubed under a picture of Hitler, said: 'One people, One state, One bag of rubble'. It is easy to dismiss these activities as mild symptoms of juvenile delinquency, but it should be remembered that many of these acts did carry very great risk.

The most organised non-conformist youth group, based in the Rhineland region, was known as the 'Edelweiss Pirates' (*Edelweisspiraten*). The members of this group were aged between 14 and 17 years. They rebelled against the rigidity of the Hitler Youth by wearing their own distinctive check shirts with an edelweiss badge on them. When they got together the Edelweiss Pirates sang pre-1933 folk songs, American hits and wicked and funny parodies of Hitler Youth songs. The Nazi regime was so concerned about the growing influence of these rebellious youth groups and street gangs they decided to suppress them. In December 1942, over 700 gang members were arrested and many of them were executed. But the anti-Nazi youth groups continued to operate and many of then teamed up with army deserters to attack the regime at the end of the war.

Humour

One way ordinary Germans could secretly express dissatisfaction with the Nazi regime was through jokes. Anti-Nazi humour was a low-level form of opposition. The Nazi leaders provided endless ammunition for jokes. Hitler jokes tended to stress his enormous power and brutality. One popular joke claimed the major difference between Chamberlain and Hitler was that while the British Prime Minister spent his weekends in the country, the Nazi leader took control of a country over the weekend. Joseph Goebbels was the subject of a great many jokes, usually revolving around the fact that he did not live up to the promised image of a master race. Goebbels had many nicknames, most notably the 'Poison Dwarf' and 'Mahatma Propagandi'. Jokes about the Hitler Youth usually focused on under-age sex, while the Nazi slogan 'Strength through Joy' gave rise to several sexual jokes. Perhaps the major source of jokes was the repressive nature of the regime. It was claimed nobody would go to the dentist in Nazi Germany because they would never be able to open their mouths in front of a stranger.

Opposition and resistance

4.1 The mood of the opposition: an underground Social Democratic Party report, south-west Germany, 1937

The number of those who consciously criticise the political objectives of the regime is very small, quite apart from the fact they cannot give expression to this criticism . . . The mood of the 'opposition' consists of an absolute conglomeration of wishes and complaints . . . Conversations with workers or with members of Church circles demonstrate how varied are the causes of the anti National Socialist mood. Some were and still are very much up in arms about the development of National Socialist Church policy and look at everything in terms of that. However, in conversations with workers the reply to the question of what they thought about the Church dispute was almost invariably: 'That doesn't interest us' . . . It becomes increasingly evident that the majority of people have two faces: one which they show to their good and reliable acquaintances; and the other for the authorities, the Party officers, the keen Nazis and for strangers. The private face shows the sharpest criticism of everything that is going on now, the official one beams with optimism and contentment.

Source: *Deutschland-Berichte der Sozialdemokratische Partei Deutschlands 1934–1940* (SOPADE reports), Frankfurt, 1979, pp. 481–82

4.2 Church opposition: a poem by Reverend Martin Niemöller, leader of the Confessional Church

When the Nazis came for the Communists
I was silent
I wasn't a Communist
When the Nazis came for the Social Democrats
I was silent
I wasn't a Social Democrat
When the Nazis came for the Trade Unionists
I was silent
I wasn't a Trade Unionist
When the Nazis came for Jews
I was silent
I wasn't a Jew
When the Nazis came for me
There was no one left
To protest

Source: A. Gill, *An honourable defeat. A history of the German resistance to Hitler*, London, 1994, p. 63

4.3 Communist opposition: a Gestapo report, Düsseldorf, 1937

Whereas until 1936 the main propaganda emphasis [of the Communists] was on distributing pamphlets, at the beginning of 1936 they switched to propaganda by word of mouth, setting up bases in factories, and advocated the so called Popular Front on the French pattern . . . It became apparent that the Communist propaganda described above was already having some success in various factories. After factory meetings at which speakers of the Labour Front [the Nazi workers' organisation] had spoken, some of whom were in fact rather clumsy in their statements, the mood of discontent among the workers was apparent in subsequent discussions. In one fairly large factory the speaker from the Labour Front greeted workers with the German [Nazi] salute, but in reply the workers only mumbled.

Source: J. Noakes and G. Pridham (eds.), *Documents on Nazism 1919–1945*, London, 1974, pp. 297–98

4.4 The manifesto of the White Rose Movement, Munich, February 1943

Fellow students! The nation is profoundly shaken by the defeat of our troops at Stalingrad. Three hundred and thirty thousand Germans have been senselessly and irresponsibly led to death and destruction through the cunning strategy of a corporal from World War 1 [Hitler]. Our Führer we thank you! The German people are growing restive. Are we to go on handing over the fate of our armies to an amateur? Are we to offer up what is left of German youth to the base instincts of the Party clique? Never. The time is coming for German youth to settle accounts with the most loathsome tyranny ever visited upon our people. In the name of German youth we demand from this Adolf Hitler government the return of our personal freedom, our most treasured possession, which he has filched away in the most despicable way. We have grown up in a state which has ruthlessly muzzled every free expression of opinion. During the critical years of our development the Hitler Youth, the SA, and the SS have tried to regiment us, to revolutionise us, to dope us. 'Ideological Education' is the name they give to their contemptible method of drowning in a flood of empty phrases every attempt we make to think for ourselves . . . For us there can only be one cry. Fight against the Party! Give up your membership of Party organisations in which all political expression has been muzzled . . . The name of Germany will be tainted for ever unless youth arises, seeking at the same time vengeance and expiation by annihilating these torturers and so help in the building of a new spiritual Europe. Fellow students! The German people look to us.

Source: Inge Scholl, *Die weisse Rose*, Frankfurt, 1952, pp. 108–10

4.5 Executions of opponents of the Nazi regime, Gestapo reports, 1940–45

Karl Robert Kreiden from Düsseldorf. A musician. While lodging in Berlin during a concert tour he tried to persuade his landlady, one Frau Ott-Monecke, to join the resistance. He described Hitler as a brute, and told Frau Ott-Monecke, a convinced National Socialist, that she had better change her ideas. She informed on him and he was tried on 3 September 1943, executed on 7 September, aged twenty-seven.

Otto Bauer, a fifty-six-year-old businessman, unguardedly said on a train in June 1942 that Germany only had two alternatives: to kill Hitler or be killed by him. He was overheard by a married couple who reported him. He was beheaded on Thursday, 16 September 1942 for fomenting discontent and unrest.

Erich Deibel. On 29 April 1940 he drew the symbol of the SPD [Social Democratic Party] – three arrows – on the wall of the lavatory in his factory, adding the words: 'Hail Freedom'. On 22 July the following year he chalked up: 'Workers! Help Russia! Strike! Up with the Communist Party of Germany!' And drew the red star and the hammer and sickle. He also allegedly listened to broadcasts from the BBC. Accused of sabotage and treason, he was executed on 15 August 1942.

Source: A. Gill, *An honourable defeat. A history of the German resistance to Hitler*, London, 1994, p. 23

4.6 The bomb plot of 20 July 1944: an eyewitness account by Otto John, a member of the resistance, of the scene at the War Ministry in Bendler-strasse, Berlin, on the day of the assassination attempt on Hitler's life in Rastenburg

On 20 July between five and six o'clock in the afternoon . . . Stauffenberg was next door busily telephoning in the chief's office. He waved to me through the half glass open door. Having nothing else to do, I watched what was going on . . . the main radio station, was spreading a report asserting that the Führer was only slightly wounded . . . For the time being there was nothing I could do but hang around and observe. In spite of the apparent turmoil, all I heard and saw, particularly snatches of Stauffenberg's telephone calls gave the impression that the whole Army was up in arms against the Nazis. It never occurred to me at that moment that they could reverse the process and stop everything. I was very impressed by Stauffenberg when he came into the ante-room and, taking a receiver from one of the girls began to issue instructions . . . I had little doubt that Himmler would try and put up some resistance through the SS, but I was sure Hitler was dead . . . I left . . . at about 8.45; strangely I looked at the clock in the near-by underground and noting it was exactly 8.53 . . . You must remember I still thought Hitler was dead, and that the radio announcement to the contrary was false . . . So I went home to tell my brother what I believed had happened at Rastenburg . . . We opened a bottle of champagne to drink to the glorious future. We were too excited to go to sleep and stayed up drinking champagne. We had the radio on, waiting for further news. The continuous recital of military music which had been going on all evening worried me slightly; I wondered why it was we had not taken over the broadcasting stations. Then, around one o'clock, Hitler spoke. It was unmistakably his voice. All our hopes vanished; we listened, breathless with sudden anxiety and bitter disappointment. What would happen now? I telephoned the Bendlerstrasse . . . But there was no reply. I realised they must have arrested Stauffenberg.

Source: R. Manvell and H. Fraenkel, *The July plot*, London, 1964, pp. 235–36

1 What impression does 4.1 give of the nature of opposition to the Nazi regime?

2 What light does 4.2 shed on opposition from church leaders to Nazi rule?

3 What does 4.3 reveal about the level of opposition to Nazi rule among industrial workers?

4 Identify the major criticisms of Nazi rule outlined in 4.4.

5 In what ways is 4.5 useful in assessing the difficulties faced by opponents of the Nazi regime?

6 What insights does 4.6 provide into the bomb plot of July 1944?

Notes and references

1 I. Kershaw, *The Nazi dictatorship. Problems and perspectives of interpretation*, 3rd edn, London, 1993, p. 150.

2 For a discussion of the problems associated with analysing resistance and opposition to Hitler see H. Deutsch, 'Symposium: New perspectives on the German resistance against National Socialism', *Central European History*, vol. 14 (1981), pp. 322–29.

3 For a detailed examination see P. Hoffman, *The German resistance to Hitler*, Cambridge, MA, 1988.

4 See E. C. Helmrich, *The German churches under Hitler*, Detroit, 1979.

5 See H. Deutsch, *The conspiracy against Hitler in the twilight of war*, Minneapolis, 1968.

6 See G. Ritter, *The German resistance: Carl Goerdeler's struggle against tyranny*, London, 1958.

7 For a detailed discussion see K. von Klemperer, *German resistance against Hitler: the search for allies abroad 1938–1945*, Oxford, 1992.

8 See J. Kramarz, *Stauffenberg*, London, 1970.

9 A. Gill, *An honourable defeat. A history of the German resistance to Hitler*, London, 1994, p. 254.

10 For a detailed discussion see A. Merson, *Communist resistance to Nazi Germany*, London, 1985.

11 Gill, *German resistance*, pp. 161–69.

12 For a very good evaluation of working-class resistance see D. Peukert, 'Working class resistance: problems and options', in D. Large (ed.), *Contending with Hitler: varieties of resistance in the Third Reich*, Cambridge, 1991.

13 Gill, *German resistance*, p. 189.

14 I. Scholl, *Students against tyranny: the resistance of the White Rose, Munich 1942–1943*, Middleton, USA, 1983.

Foreign policy: Hitler's road to war, 1933–39

Adolf Hitler devoted most of his attention to foreign policy. According to Göring: 'Foreign policy above all was the Führer's very own realm. By that I mean to say that foreign policy on the one hand, and the leadership of the Armed forces on the other, enlisted the Führer's greatest interest and were his main activity. He busied himself exceptionally with the details in both these spheres.'[1]

The central objective of German foreign policy between 1918 and 1933 was to revise 'the slave treaty' (the Treaty of Versailles). In the mid-1920s Gustav Stresemann, the German Foreign Minister, aimed to work in a peaceful and constructive manner with the major wartime allies (Britain, France and Italy) in order to fulfil German obligations under the treaty in the hope that this would lead to concessions. Stresemann's conciliatory policy eased European tensions, most notably resulting in the signing of the Locarno Treaties (1925), which guaranteed the western frontiers laid down by Versailles and brought Germany into the League of Nations in 1926. Germany also gained some modification to the terms of Versailles. In 1930, allied troops left Germany; the payment of reparations (one of the most hated clauses of Versailles) were reduced under the Young Plan (1929) and effectively dropped at the Lausanne Conference (1932).

The death of Stresemann on 3 October 1929 ended this conciliatory approach. From 1930 to 1933 – when Germany was ruled by presidential decree – German foreign policy moved away from a policy of peaceful collaboration with the allies to revise Versailles towards a revisionist policy of 'going it alone'. In March 1931, Chancellor Heinrich Brüning proposed a customs union with Austria, but this was blocked by allied pressure. In July 1932, von Papen gave the go-ahead for a secret rearmament programme. It now seems apparent that German foreign policy was in a state of transition from 1930 to 1933, clearly leading in the direction of revising the Treaty of Versailles by unilateral action.

On coming to power in 1933, Hitler was determined to accelerate this trend. Most of Hitler's actions in foreign policy from 1933 to 1939 were linked to German grievances over Versailles. But Hitler's foreign policy aims went way beyond a mere revision of the Versailles Treaty. In a speech to army officers on 3 February 1933, Hitler said the armed forces would undertake a programme of expansion designed to make Germany the major military power in Europe by 1938, with the ultimate objective of gaining *Lebensraum* in the east at the expense of the Soviet Union.

Hitler moves cautiously

In 1933, Germany was in a very weak economic and military position. Hitler knew he had to proceed with extreme caution. In the early years of Nazi rule, he gave a masterly impression in his speeches of being a man of sweet reasonableness, concerned only with equal treatment for Germany. On 17 May 1933, for example, Hitler claimed that Germany was the only nation disarmed and he called on other powers to follow suit.[2] The British government was very impressed by Hitler's 'peaceful intentions'. At the World Disarmament Conference, Ramsay MacDonald, the British Prime Minister, proposed a reduction in the French army from 500,000 to 200,000 and an increase in the German army from 100,000 to 200,000. The French government rejected this proposal. On 14 October 1933, Hitler withdrew Germany from the Disarmament Conference and also from the League of Nations, claiming neither body could treat Germany equally. This move allowed Hitler to push ahead with rearmament and opened the way for Germany to engage in bilateral diplomacy.

The first bilateral treaty was a non-aggression pact with Poland in January 1934. The agreement was signed by Hitler in the face of strong opposition from the Foreign Ministry and many Nazi activists. It was greeted with astonishment outside Germany. Since 1919, German foreign policy had followed a strong anti-Polish line, because Poland had gained Upper Silesia, economic control over Danzig and a 'Polish corridor', a strip of land to the sea, which cut off east Prussia from the rest of Germany, under the terms of Versailles. It seemed that Hitler was abandoning these claims, but in reality the agreement with Poland was an act of calculated duplicity. It was designed by Hitler to give the false impression that Germany had peaceful intentions in eastern Europe. Ultimately, an independent Poland had no place in Hitler's foreign policy plans, but for the moment tension with Poland was eased, and French influence in eastern Europe weakened.

The first setback to Hitler's carefully cultivated image as peace seeker came in July 1934, when the Austrian Nazi Party attempted a coup d'état against the Austrian government. On 25 July 1934, Nazi hot-heads broke into the office of the Austrian Chancellor, Engelbert Dollfuss – and killed him. But the murder of Dollfuss did not lead to the overthrow of the Austrian government, only to outrage against Hitler in most European capitals. It was widely believed that Hitler had planned the coup, but he denied any involvement. Mussolini, the Italian dictator, was so outraged by the murder of Dollfuss that he sent troops to the Austrian border and pledged to aid Austria in the event of a German attack. In a damage-limitation exercise, Hitler handed over the leaders of the coup to the Austrian authorities. The incident revealed Germany was still diplomatically isolated in Europe and not yet militarily strong enough to adopt a bolder position. Mussolini's outrage over the Dollfuss affair led to closer Franco-Italian co-operation. In January 1935, a Franco-Italian agreement was signed which further emphasised the diplomatic isolation of Nazi Germany.

German rearmament

In the early months of 1935, German armed forces were expanding rapidly. This encouraged Hitler to adopt a bolder course. In January 1935, he gained a major foreign policy success when over 90 per cent of voters in the Saar region – which had been under the control of a League of Nations commission since 1919 – agreed to return to Germany. On 11 March 1935, Hitler announced his first major foreign policy 'surprise': a German air-force (prohibited by the Treaty of Versailles) already existed. On 16 March came another shock: the German army was already 240,000 strong and conscription was to be introduced from that day, which could expand it to 36 divisions, numbering 550,000 troops. At the same time, Hitler announced Germany no longer accepted the military restrictions of Versailles.

Stresa Front

The leaders of Britain, France and Italy met at Stresa between 11 and 14 April 1935 to discuss their response to these worrying developments. They produced a strong joint declaration condemning Germany's unilateral breach of the arms limits set by Versailles and expressed a determination to prevent any attempt to undermine Austrian independence. On 17 April, the League of Nations passed a motion of censure against the unilateral breaches by Germany of the military clauses of Versailles. The news of German rearmament prompted the French government to improve Franco-Soviet relations. On 2 May 1935, a treaty of mutual assistance was agreed between France and the Soviet Union, with each party promising to aid each other in the event of an unprovoked attract. On 16 May 1935, France and the Soviet Union signed a similar agreement with Czechoslovakia. But the Franco–Soviet–Czech agreement contained a subtle get-out clause for the two major powers: France had to be actively helping the Czechs in the event of an unprovoked attack for the Soviet Union to become actively involved. These strong diplomatic initiatives by France, Britain, Italy, the Soviet Union and Czechoslovakia represent the high-point of allied unity to prevent a German military revival.

Anglo-German naval agreement

It was not long before the Stresa Front was undermined. The British government, unhappy about the decision of the French government to enter a bilateral agreement with the Soviet Union, decided to improve Anglo-German relations. On 18 June 1935 – the 120th anniversary of the Battle of Waterloo – the British government, without consulting the French, signed a bilateral naval agreement with Nazi Germany which limited German shipbuilding to 35 per cent of the strength of the Royal Navy and recognised Germany's right to build submarines.[3] After hearing the Anglo-German naval agreement had been signed, Hitler described it as 'the happiest day of my life'.[4]

The Abyssinian crisis

In October 1935, the unity of the Stresa Front was shattered when Italy invaded Abyssinia (modern-day Ethiopia). The attack was not unexpected: Italy had sought revenge against Abyssinia ever since the humiliating Italian defeat at Adwa in 1896. The attack came at a particularly bad time for Stanley Baldwin, the British Prime Minister, whose national government was fighting a general election pledged to uphold the principles of collective security through the League of Nations. The British government was now placed in the deeply embarrassing position of matching strong words with action. Samuel Hoare, the British Foreign Secretary, supported the introduction of economic sanctions against Italy, and these were adopted by the League of Nations.[5]

But the French government did not really want to punish Mussolini too harshly, just in case the Italian dictator decided to move closer to Hitler. Pierre Laval, the French Foreign Minister, met Hoare in Paris on 7 December 1935 with the intention of finding some way to ease the diplomatic pressure on Mussolini. Hoare and Laval secretly agreed to Italy gaining most of Abyssinia – except for a small strip of land along the coast. But the Hoare–Laval Pact was leaked to the press, causing profound political embarrassment. Hoare was forced to resign and Laval's coalition government fell from office. The Abyssinian crisis showed that the French and British governments paid lip service to the ideals of the League in public while being secretly prepared to abandon those principles when they went behind closed doors. More alarmingly, the affair did push Mussolini into diplomatic isolation and allowed Hitler to bring him into the Nazi orbit. Above all, the Abyssinian crisis deeply wounded the authority of the League of Nations.

The occupation of the Rhineland

It was against this background that Hitler decided to embark on his next major surprise in foreign affairs. On 7 March 1936, German troops reoccupied the Rhineland – an area demilitarised under the terms of Versailles.[6] The French and British governments agreed to take no military action. Hitler's march into the Rhineland killed the Locarno Treaties and further undermined the authority of the League of Nations. The decision to send troops into the Rhineland was Hitler's alone, taken against the advice of the army high command, which feared French military retaliation, for which the German army was not really prepared. Hitler decided to occupy the Rhineland because he thought that in the wake of the diplomatic upheaval caused by the Italian invasion of Abyssinia, neither France nor Britain would act. Hitler's political judgement proved accurate.

The Spanish Civil War

The Rhineland crisis soon blew over. It was quickly followed by the outbreak of the Spanish Civil War. The Civil War grew out of a crisis in another fragile democracy. In February 1936, the Nationalists became the largest party in the

Cortes (Spanish parliament), but a Popular Front of socialists, liberals and Communists joined together to prevent them taking office. A group of right-wing army officers, led by General Franco, commander of the Spanish army in Morocco, started a rebellion in July 1936. The Spanish Civil War was presented as a struggle between Fascism and democracy. Mussolini and Hitler provided substantial military support to Franco and the rebel Nationalists. The British and French governments both adopted a policy of 'non-intervention', which involved giving no military support to either side. The Soviet Union gave some limited support to the Communists engaged in the struggle.[7]

Two dictators get together. Hitler and Mussolini review troops in Munich in 1937.

The Spanish Civil War helped Hitler's own foreign policy aims in a number of ways:

1 it diverted attention from the rapid progress of German rearmament;
2 it provided a valuable training ground for the German air-force;
3 it allowed Hitler an opportunity to give vent to his anti-Communism;
4 it allowed Germany to build close relations with Italy.

Relations with Italy, Japan and Britain

During the remainder of 1936, Hitler concluded two important diplomatic agreements. In October, the Rome–Berlin axis was signed, which emphasised Mussolini's alienation from the British and French governments.[8] On 25 November, Germany signed the Anti-Comintern pact with Japan, which pledged both countries to fight the spread of Communism.[9] By the end of 1936, Hitler's popularity, bolstered by the remilitarisation of the Rhineland and the signing of the Rome–Berlin axis, stood at an all-time high.

Hitler gives up hope of an Anglo-German alliance

In spite of the development of close relations with Italy, Hitler had not abandoned his long-cherished dream of an Anglo-German alliance. In March 1936, Hitler appointed Joachim von Ribbentrop, a committed Nazi, as ambassador to London, with the purpose of surveying the possibility of an alliance. Von Ribbentrop talked to all the leading appeasers in the British government, but came to the conclusion that Britain was not prepared to sign the alliance Hitler wanted, which was for Britain to give Germany a 'free hand' in eastern Europe in return for a guarantee of the British Empire. On hearing this news from von Ribbentrop, Hitler started to become disillusioned with the idea of an Anglo-German alliance and began to realise he may have to pursue his foreign policy aims with Britain as a possible antagonist in a future war.

At the same time that Hitler was becoming disillusioned with the prospects of an alliance with Britain, Neville Chamberlain, who became British Prime Minister in May 1937, was becoming very optimistic about his own plan to improve Anglo-German relations. Chamberlain was deeply alarmed by the growth of tension in Europe and was stubbornly confident enough to believe he could prevent war through determined and energetic diplomatic efforts. Chamberlain decided to attempt to prevent war through a policy known as appeasement.[10] The aim of this policy was to satisfy the grievances of Germany and Italy left behind by the 1919 peace settlement, in the hope this would encourage Hitler and Mussolini to participate in a new general settlement of European problems. What Chamberlain could not offer was a separate Anglo-German alliance, or a blank cheque for German domination of Europe – which were the only terms Hitler was willing to accept. Given the differing aims of Chamberlain and Hitler, the policy of appeasement could never have worked. In November 1937, Chamberlain sent Lord Halifax on a semi-official trip to meet the Nazi leader. Halifax informed Hitler that the British government was prepared to support any legitimate German claims over Austria and Czecho-slovakia, provided they were negotiated peacefully. Hitler once again emphasised that what he most wanted from the British government was a 'free hand' for Germany to deal with problems in eastern Europe in any way Hitler liked.

The Hossbach memorandum

In November 1937, Hitler was already moving away from the idea of an Anglo-German alliance and regarded the Halifax visit as an unwelcome intrusion into his own plans. On 5 November, Hitler summoned a select group of leading military and foreign policy figures to discuss his future strategy and aims. A record of what took place was kept by Colonel Friedrich Hossbach, partly from memory, and this became known as the 'Hossbach memorandum'. Hitler told the meeting that the chief aim of German foreign policy was 'conquest' of 'living space', which had to be achieved 'by force' between 1943 and 1945, while Germany still enjoyed a military advantage. Hitler also made it plain that Austria and Czechoslovakia would have to be seized. He predicted that these actions might provoke a war with France and Britain, which he now described as 'two hate inspired antagonists', but he was willing to risk a war to achieve his objectives.[11] A great deal has been made of the significance of this meeting, with some historians viewing it as evidence of a firm plan for a war against Britain and France (the very war which broke out in September 1939), while others have attempted to play down its importance, suggesting it was merely a 'pep talk' to the generals to persuade them to push ahead with rearmament.

Hitler takes charge of the army

It now seems clear that the Hossbach memorandum can be regarded as marking the beginning of a much bolder era of German foreign policy. Early in 1938, Hitler purged a number of conservatives from influential positions in the army and the Foreign Office. General von Blomberg, the Minister of War, and Colonel-General von Fritsch, army commander-in-chief, who had both expressed opposition to Hitler's plans for war with Britain and France at the Hossbach meeting, were removed from office. At the same time, von Neurath, the 'moderate' German Foreign Minister, was replaced by the 'radical' and increasingly anti-British von Ribbentrop. To strengthen his grip over the army further, Hitler abolished the post of Minister of War, took on the role of supreme commander of the armed forces and created a new high command of the armed forces (*Oberkommando der Wehrmacht*), under the leadership of the loyal and subservient General Wilhelm Keitel. In the same reshuffle, Göring was made a field marshal, putting him at a higher rank than all the other commanders-in-chief. These changes gave Hitler much greater control over the armed forces and foreign policy than he had ever enjoyed before. As von Fritsch put it: 'This man, Hitler, is Germany's destiny for good or evil. If he now goes over the abyss, he will drag us all down with him. There is nothing we can do.'[12]

The Anschluss

Following these changes, the tension in European politics greatly intensified. The first major new initiative by Hitler on foreign policy was the seizure of Austria. Goebbels, in his diary, recorded that Hitler intended to settle the Anschluss by force, but gives no firm date.[13] The German army had no military plans for an invasion of Austria. It seems that Hitler hoped the Austrian Nazis might be able to engineer a peaceful take-over. In January 1938, Kurt von Schuschnigg, the Austrian leader, requested a meeting with Hitler to ask him to persuade the Austrian Nazis to stop engaging in disruptive activities. On 12 February 1938, Hitler did meet Schuschnigg, but used the meeting to bully him into making further concessions to the disruptive Austrian Nazis, including the inclusion of two Nazis in the Austrian cabinet, one of whom was to take charge of internal security. Quite bravely, or foolishly, Schuschnigg, on his return to Vienna, decided to call a referendum which asked voters to support Austrian independence. But this move outraged Hitler, who put more pressure on Schuschnigg and he resigned on 11 March 1938 in favour of a pro-Nazi government, led by Arthur Seyss-Inquart, whose first act as Austrian leader was to 'invite' Hitler to occupy Austria. On 12 March 1938, German troops entered Austria; a few hours later Hitler crossed the border. He was greeted in Linz by a quite delirious reception which so moved him that he decided – on the spur of the moment – to integrate Austria into the German Reich. The next day, Hitler drove in triumph through the streets of Vienna. The achievement of the Anschluss, without firing a shot, was a victory parade – not an invasion, even though it was regarded as an occupation throughout the rest of the world. It was really a stunning example of Hitler's impulsive opportunism in foreign affairs. France, without a government when the Anschluss took place, took no action. Chamberlain issued a polite protest, but quickly accepted the Nazi take-over in Austria as an accomplished fact. As a result of the Anschluss, German dominance over central Europe was a fact of life and Czechoslovakia was under grave threat.

The Czech crisis

For the remainder of 1938, the crisis over Czechoslovakia was the dominant issue in European relations. Czechoslovakia, a democratic state, created by the peace settlement of 1919, contained a number of diverse nationalities, including 3.5 million German-speakers living in a border region called the Sudetenland. For years, Hitler had given financial support to the pro-Nazi Sudeten German Party, led by Konrad Henlein. Hitler now portrayed himself as the unlikely defender of this 'oppressed minority'. The Czech crisis was made more serious by the existence of a number of diplomatic arrangements. Czechoslovakia had diplomatic agreements with France and the Soviet Union which promised military support in the event of a military attack. This meant the Czech crisis held out the possibility of a major European war. The Czech position was not as secure in reality as it appeared on paper. The agreement with the Soviet Union became operative only if France acted first to defend Czech territory.

The Czech position was made worse by the attitude of Chamberlain, who was quite prepared to see Germany annex the Sudetenland provided this was achieved through peaceful negotiation. In May 1938, news spread of menacing German troop movements near the Czech border. In response, the Czech, French, Soviet and British governments promised to resist an unprovoked German attack. Hitler denied he was planning an invasion of Czechoslovakia (which appears to be true). The 'May crisis', interpreted across Europe as a major climb-down by Hitler, served only to make the Nazi dictator decide to set a firm date to 'crush Czechoslovakia by force' – 1 October 1938.

In the summer of 1938, the crisis over Czechoslovakia mounted. A British attempt to mediate between the Czech government and the Sudeten German Party, undertaken by Lord Runciman, ended in failure. The Czech government offered every possible concession to Henlein, but the Sudeten leader was under strict orders from Hitler to keep asking for more. On 12 September 1938, Hitler, speaking at the annual Nuremberg rally of the Nazi Party, demanded self-determination for the Sudeten Germans and appeared to threaten war. At this point, Chamberlain, in a remarkable display of personal diplomacy, decided to visit Hitler in an attempt to avert a European war.

The impact of Chamberlain

On 15 September 1938, Chamberlain made a seven-hour flight, followed by a three-hour car journey, to meet Hitler at Berchtesgaden. Hitler told Chamberlain he wanted the Sudetenland incorporated into Germany or there would be war. Hitler assumed that Chamberlain had no chance of persuading the Czechs to transfer the Sudetenland to Germany peacefully. He miscalculated the exceptional determination of Chamberlain to find a peaceful solution. In less than a week, Chamberlain persuaded the French and coerced the Czech government into accepting Hitler's demands. On 22 September 1938, Chamberlain flew back to Germany to meet Hitler at Godesberg to tell him the good news. At the second meeting, Hitler made new demands, including an immediate occupation of the Sudetenland. Czechs who wanted to leave the Sudetenland would be allowed to take only a single suitcase of clothing with them. Chamberlain was prepared to accept the 'Godesberg memorandum', but the cabinet, the French and Czech government would not.

The Munich agreement

It now seemed the nerve-jangling Czech crisis would lead to a European war. It was Mussolini, egged on by Chamberlain, who persuaded Hitler to accept a negotiated settlement. The Munich agreement was signed on 30 September 1938 by Hitler (Germany), Chamberlain (Britain), Mussolini (Italy) and Daladier (France). The agreement enabled Hitler to incorporate the Sudetenland into Nazi Germany by 10 October 1938. A vague promise was given by the four powers to guarantee the territory of the rest of Czechoslovakia – but it was never ratified. The Munich agreement was not very different from the Godesberg memorandum.

In a separate agreement, Chamberlain persuaded Hitler to sign a declaration of Anglo-German friendship, which claimed the Munich agreement was 'symbolic of the desire of our two peoples never to go to war with one another again'. This was the famous 'piece of paper' which Chamberlain waved triumphantly above his head when he returned to an enthusiastic welcome at Heston Airport. The Czech government was left outside the conference room in which the Munich agreement was signed; the Soviet Union was not even invited. The total rejection of Soviet help by Britain, France and Czechoslovakia during the Czech crisis helped to convince Stalin that the western powers were not interested in upholding collective security and were not greatly alarmed by Hitler's advance in eastern Europe.

But Hitler was not satisfied with the Munich settlement. 'That senile old rascal Chamberlain,' Hitler fumed, 'has spoiled my entry into Prague.'[14] In the days following Munich, Hitler's mood was black and depressed. He had wanted to invade Czechoslovakia by force all along, in spite of the reluctance of his army general staff, and he felt cheated of a military victory. Only three weeks after Munich, Hitler issued a directive to the army to make preparations 'to liquidate the remainder of Czechoslovakia'.[15]

The aftermath of Munich

Following the Munich agreement, most of the small powers in eastern Europe tried to strengthen their economic and political ties with Nazi Germany. Romania signed a trade agreement in December 1938 guaranteeing oil supplies to Germany, Hungary joined the anti-Comintern pact and Yugoslavia also signed a trade agreement. The only small country in eastern Europe which did not go out of its way to court Hitler in the aftermath of Munich was Poland. In the winter of 1938–39, von Ribbentrop made energetic efforts to persuade Poland to agree to the return of Danzig, another German loss under the Treaty of Versailles, and to join an anti-Soviet alliance. But the Polish government refused to accede to these German demands.

Another feature of German foreign policy after Munich was its distinctly anti-British tone. In speeches, Hitler included antagonistic tirades against 'warmongers' in Britain and claimed he did not want 'umbrella-carrying politicians' (an obvious reference to Chamberlain) interfering in European problems.

In the early months of 1939, the press throughout the world was full of rumours concerning Hitler's 'next move'. It seemed clear that he was waiting for the right moment to occupy Czechoslovakia. In the meantime, the British government drew closer to France. On 6 February 1939, Chamberlain announced that any threat to French interests would immediately bring forth British support. This amounted to an Anglo-French alliance. At the same time, preparations were made to send a large British expeditionary force to France in the event of war.

The occupation of Czechoslovakia

On 15 March 1939, German troops occupied the remainder of Czechoslovakia, ostensibly to 'restore order'. Hitler and his army drove through the streets of Prague, this time past a silent, mournful and depressed crowd of Czechs, most of whom were crying, not cheering. No one outside Germany would smile any more when they saw Hitler's tanks. Hitler's silent car ride through the streets of Prague left him cold and he took very little interest in Czechoslovakia thereafter. The British and French governments decided not to take any military action, giving the limp excuse that because the Czech government fell before German troops invaded, the guarantee given at Munich did not apply. The occupation of Czechoslovakia killed Chamberlain's hopes that Hitler could be successfully appeased by concessions alone.

Poland under threat

It seemed every small country in Europe was now at the mercy of Hitler's dynamic foreign policy. On 22 March 1938, Lithuania was brought under Nazi rule. The next day, the disputed city of Memel, on the border of east Prussia, was occupied by German troops. Hitler urged Poland to come to an agreement with Germany over Danzig and the Polish corridor. The Polish government refused to become the next item on Hitler's shopping list of territorial acquisitions.

On 31 March 1939, the British government (supported by the French government) offered support to Poland in the event of an unprovoked attack, in a move designed to warn Hitler of the consequences of further aggression. Hitler was 'absolutely amazed' at the Polish decision to join an alliance with Britain and France. The Polish government and people were to pay a very heavy price in blood for their decision to defy the Nazi dictator. On 3 April 1939, Hitler ordered 'Operation White' – the code name for the attack on Poland – set to begin on 1 September 1939.

Hitler was not convinced the western allies would go to war to save Poland and he spent the summer keeping up the pressure on Poland, while at the same time seizing every opportunity to weaken Anglo-French resolve. On 22 May 1939, Hitler and Mussolini signed the 'Pact of Steel', a ten-year alliance. The next day, Hitler told the army high command to prepare to 'attack Poland at the earliest opportunity'. By this stage, Hitler had come to realise that Britain 'is our enemy' and that a showdown with the British Empire was 'a matter of life and death'.

The prelude to the Nazi–Soviet pact

The German threat to Poland in the summer of 1939 greatly enhanced the diplomatic and strategic importance of the Soviet Union. Chamberlain, a lifelong anti-Communist, had a very low opinion of Soviet military power and dithered over the benefits of an Anglo-Soviet alliance. The Polish government seemed to prefer a German attack to military assistance from the Red Army.

Only with extreme reluctance did Chamberlain open negotiations for an Anglo-Soviet alliance during the summer of 1939. On the British side, the negotiations were conducted by a very lowly Admiralty figure (Admiral Sir Reginald Aylmer Ranfurly Plunkett-Ernle-Erle-Drax), who did not depart for the Soviet Union until 5 August 1939, on board a merchant ship which took six days to arrive. The Soviet authorities were amazed to learn when Drax arrived that he did not have full powers to sign an alliance, which meant that even if an agreement were reached, there would be a further agonising delay before the actual treaty was signed. The talks went on for a week, but they collapsed on 19 August 1939 because the Polish government refused to allow Soviet troops on Polish soil in the event of war. The slow approach which the British government adopted towards the negotiations proved a monumental error.

Hitler saw the delay as a huge diplomatic opportunity. The British government assumed Hitler's hatred of Communism and Stalin's hostility to Fascism made a Nazi–Soviet pact an impossibility. They ignored Hitler's flexibility in pursuit of his immediate foreign policy aims and Stalin's supreme political shrewdness. Hitler saw a pact with Stalin as the best way of getting France and Britain to back out of the guarantee to Poland, while Stalin decided a pact with Hitler was the best diplomatic deal on offer.[16] It would prevent the Soviet Union from going to war, not fully prepared, to defend a country which had consistently rejected all offers of Soviet military aid.

The Nazi–Soviet pact was signed on 23 August 1939. A secret clause in the treaty allowed Stalin to recapture Latvia, Lithuania and Estonia, which had been seized by Poland during the Russian Civil War. Stalin knew the Nazi–Soviet pact was a politically expedient means of delaying the bitter racial war Hitler had in mind for the Soviet people and he made no attempt to disguise the fact. Of all the contemporary leaders, Stalin was the only one Hitler truly admired. He would often say to his close aides: 'That fellow Stalin is a brute, but you really must admit, he's an extraordinary fellow.'[17]

The outbreak of the Second World War

After the signing of the Nazi–Soviet pact, Hitler felt certain that Chamberlain would exert pressure on Poland to accede to his demands. But Chamberlain expressed a clear determination to stand by Poland in the event of a German attack. On 25 August 1939, Hitler delayed his attack on Poland (finally set for 26 August) to offer Britain a guarantee of the British Empire in return for British help to negotiate an agreement over the Danzig question. Hitler's offer was communicated to the Polish government, but Polish ministers refused to negotiate with the Nazi regime. At dawn on 1 September 1939, Germany attacked Poland. On 3 September 1939, Britain at 11 a.m. and France at 5 p.m. finally declared war on Germany. Italy, in spite of all Mussolini's warlike posturing, decided to remain neutral. Hence, Hitler began the Second World War against Britain, which he had always wanted to be a German ally, and with the Soviet Union, a nation he wanted to annihilate, as a diplomatic partner. Hitler had clearly got his war, but it was not the war he had originally wanted or planned.

Document case study
Hitler's road to war, 1933–39

5.1 Hitler's views on foreign policy, 1934

The struggle against Versailles is the means, but not the end of my policy. I am not in the least interested in the former frontiers of the Reich. The re-creation of pre-war Germany is not a task worthy of our revolution . . . we have to proceed step by step, so that no one will impede our advance. How to do this I don't yet know. But that it will be done is guaranteed by Britain's lack of firmness and France's internal disunity . . . Britain needs a strong Germany. Britain and France will never make common cause against Germany . . . I shall do everything in my power to prevent co-operation between Britain and France. If I succeed in bringing in Italy and Britain to our side, the first part of our struggle for power will be greatly facilitated . . . I must gain space for Germany, space big enough to enable us to defend ourselves against a military coalition. In peacetime we can manage. But in war the important thing is freedom of action, for in war one is mortally dependent on the outside world. Our dependence on foreign trade without even an ocean coastline would condemn us eternally to the position of a politically dependent nation . . . We need space . . . to make us independent of every possible political grouping and alliance. In the east we must have the mastery as far as the Caucasus and Iran. In the west, we need the French coast. We need Flanders and Holland. Above all we need Sweden . . . We cannot, like Bismarck, limit ourselves to national aims. We must rule Europe or fall apart as a nation.

Source: H. Rauschning, *Hitler speaks: a series of conversations with Adolf Hitler on his real aims*, London, 1940, pp. 121–26

5.2 Hitler's views on the occupation of the Rhineland, 1936

Germany no longer feels bound by the Locarno Treaty. In the interests of the primitive rights of its people to the security of their frontier and the safeguarding of their defence, the German government has re-established as from today, the absolute and unrestricted sovereignty of the Reich in the demilitarized zone . . . In this historic hour, when, in the Reich's western provinces German troops are at this minute marching into their future peacetime garrisons, we all unite in two sacred cows . . . First, we swear to yield to no force whatever in restoration of the honour of our people . . . Second, we pledge that now, more than ever, we shall strive for an understanding between the European peoples, especially with our western neighbour nations . . . We have no territorial demands to make in Europe!

Source: W. Shirer, *The rise and fall of the Third Reich*, London, 1960, pp. 291–92

5.3 Hitler's secret speech to the German press, 1938

It has been the pressure of circumstances that has made me talk of peace for decades on end. For only by repeatedly emphasizing the German wish for peace and its peaceful intentions could I hope gradually to secure freedom for the German people and to provide it with the right kind of armaments which have always been the indispensable prerequisite for any further move. Such a peace propaganda lasting over a decade has necessarily had its questionable side effects. For many people may thereby easily be led to think that the existing regime is actually identical with the resolution and the wish to preserve peace at any cost.

Source: A. Adamthwaite, *The making of the Second World War*, London, 1977, p. 200

5.4 Hitler reviews his foreign policy for the army generals, February 1939

All our actions during 1938 represent only the logical extension of the decisions which began to be realised in 1933. It is not the case that during this year of 1938 – let us say – a particular action occurred which was not previously envisaged. On the contrary, all the individual decisions which have been realised since 1933 are not the result of momentary considerations but represent the implementation of a previously existing plan, though, perhaps not exactly according to the schedule which was envisaged. For example, in 1933 I was not exactly certain when the withdrawal from the League of Nations would occur. However, it was clear that this withdrawal had to be the first step towards Germany's revival . . . We could see from the start that the next step would have to be rearmament without the permission of foreign countries . . . It was further obvious that, after a certain period of rearmament, Germany would have to take the daring step of proclaiming its freedom from restrictions from rearmament. At the beginning, naturally one could not foresee the right moment for this step. Finally, it was further clear that every step must first involve the remilitarization of the Rhineland. The date for this was in fact envisaged as being one year later: I did not think I would carry it out until 1937. The circumstances at the time made it seem appropriate to carry it out as early as 1936. It was also quite obvious that the Austrian and Czech problems would have to be solved in order further to strengthen Germany's political and, in particular, her strategic position. To start with I was not sure whether both problems ought to be or could be solved simultaneously or whether one should deal first with the question of Czechoslovakia or with the Austrian question. There was no doubt these questions would have to be solved, and so all these decisions were not ideas which were realised at the moment of their conception, but were long made plans which I was determined to realize the moment I thought the circumstances at the time were favourable.

Source: J. Noakes and G. Pridham (eds.), *Nazism 1919–1945. A documentary reader, Vol. 3: Foreign policy, war and racial extermination*, Exeter, 1988, p. 725

5.5 Hitler speaks to the generals, May 1939

After six years the present position is as follows:
With minor exceptions German national unification has been achieved. Further successes cannot be achieved without bloodshed. Poland will always be on the side of our adversaries. Despite the friendship agreement Poland has always intended to exploit every opportunity against us. Danzig is not the objective. It is a matter of expanding our living space in the east, of making our food supplies secure, and of solving the problem of the Baltic states. To provide sufficient food you must have sparsely settled areas. This is fertile soil, whose surpluses will be very much increased by German, thorough management . . . The Polish regime will not resist pressure from Russia. Poland sees danger in a German victory in the west and will try and deprive us of our victory. There is therefore no question of sparing Poland, and the decision remains to attack Poland at the first suitable opportunity. We cannot expect a repetition of Czechoslovakia. There will be fighting. The task is to isolate Poland. Success in isolating her will be decisive . . . Basic principle: conflict with Poland, beginning with attack on Poland, will be successful only if the west keeps out. If that is impossible, then it is better to attack the west and finish off Poland at the same time.

Source: *Documents on German foreign policy, 1918–1945*, series D, vol. VI, no. 433, London, 1956

5.6 Hitler explains his decision to sign the Nazi–Soviet pact, August 1939

Since the autumn of 1938 and since I have realised Japan will not go with us unconditionally and that Mussolini is endangered by that nitwit of a King and the treacherous scoundrel of a Crown Prince, I decided to go with Stalin. After all there are only three great statesmen in the world, Stalin, I and Mussolini. Mussolini is the weakest, for he has been able to break the power of neither the crown nor of the Church. Stalin and I are the only ones who visualize the future. So in a few weeks I shall stretch out my hand to Stalin at the common frontier and with him undertake to redistribute the world . . . After Stalin's death – he is a very sick man – we will break the Soviet Union. Then will begin the dawn of the German rule of the earth.

Source: E. L. Woodward and R. Butler (eds.), *Documents on British foreign policy 1919–1939*, 3rd series, vol. VII, no. 314, London, 1954

Document case-study questions

1 Identify the main features of Hitler's foreign policy aims as outlined in 5.1.
2 Assess the historical significance of Hitler's comments in 5.2.
3 Summarise what 5.3 tells us about Hitler's public speeches on foreign policy.
4 What insights does 5.4 provide into Hitler's approach to foreign policy from 1933 to 1939?
5 What reservations would have you have regarding 5.4 as historical evidence?
6 What does 5.5 tell us about Hitler's foreign policy in 1939?

7 Assess the value of 5.6 in explaining Hitler's decision to sign the Nazi–Soviet pact.

Notes and references

1 A. Bullock, *Hitler. A study of tyranny*, revised edn, London, 1964, p. 313.

2 *Ibid.*, p. 321.

3 See H. H. Hall, 'The origins of the Anglo-German naval agreement', *Historical Journal*, vol. 17 (1976).

4 Hitler saw the naval agreement as the prelude to the signing of an Anglo-German alliance, whereby Hitler would guarantee the British Empire in return for a 'free hand' in Europe. Hitler's desire for an agreement with Britain on these terms was a key aim of his foreign policy during the late 1920s and this desire remained strong during the 1930s. It was after 1937, largely under the influence of von Ribbentrop, that Hitler came to realise such an agreement was not possible.

5 Economic sanctions against Italy were completely ineffective and were quietly dropped in July 1936.

6 For a detailed discussion see C. T. Emerson, *The Rhineland crisis, 7 March 1936*, London, 1977.

7 The standard work on the conflict in Spain is H. Thomas, *The Spanish Civil War*, London, 1977.

8 The Spanish Civil War resulted in a victory for the Nationalist forces under Franco in 1939, but Spain remained neutral during the Second World War.

9 In 1937, Italy also joined the Anti-Comintern pact.

10 For a detailed examination see F. McDonough, *Neville Chamberlain, appeasement and the British road to war*, Manchester, 1998.

11 *Documents on German foreign policy, 1918–45*, series D, vol. I, London, 1949–82.

12 Bullock, *Hitler*, p. 420.

13 I. Kershaw, *The Nazi dictatorship. Problems and perspectives of interpretation*, 3rd edn, London, 1993, p. 120.

14 D. C. Watt, *How war came. The immediate origins of the Second World War*, London, 1989, p. 30.

15 Bullock, *Hitler*, p. 473.

16 See G. Roberts, 'The Soviet decision for a pact with Germany', *Soviet Studies*, vol. 44 (1992).

17 J. Toland, *Adolf Hitler*, New York, 1976, p. 821.

6 Hitler at war, 1939–45

The role Nazi Germany played in the Second World War can be divided into four phases. The first runs from the invasion of Poland in September 1939 to the fall of France in June 1940. In this period, the German armed forces enjoyed an unbroken string of military victories, which placed Nazi Germany in control of most of western and central Europe. The second phase runs from June 1940 to June 1941, when Britain fought alone against Nazi Germany and survived invasion during the Battle of Britain. The third phase runs from the beginning of the German attack on the Soviet Union in June 1941 to the first major defeat of the German army, at Stalingrad in February 1943. During this period, the Second World War became a truly global conflict. The final phase of Hitler's war runs from the German defeat at Stalingrad to ultimate defeat in May 1945. In this final phase of the war, Nazi Germany proved incapable of defeating the combined strength of the three largest anti-Nazi allies – the Soviet Union, the USA and Britain.

Hitler as war lord

During the Second World War, German military strategy was conducted by Hitler, whose reputation as a military commander has received widespread criticism. According to General Erich von Manstein, Hitler put the power of his own will above the strategic advice of his generals, with disastrous conse-quences.[1] Similarly, General Franz Halder claimed that Hitler destroyed a well-organised military command system with 'a mystical conviction of his own infallibility'.[2] Hitler was not ignorant of military matters, but he had no experience of commanding large armies and proved unwilling to listen to information – or expert advice – which contradicted his own opinions. Generals who disagreed with Hitler found themselves moved or replaced.

In the early stage of the war, the swift German victories gave Hitler enormous self-confidence in his powers as a military strategist. But when the military campaign in the Soviet Union started to flounder in 1942–43, Hitler went on believing a German victory was still possible. He never allowed the facts to get in the way of his own view of events. For example, when Halder informed him of intelligence information indicating the Soviet Union was producing 1,200 new tanks a month in the summer of 1942, Hitler thumped the table with his fist and shouted 'Russia is dead.'[3]

Another severe weakness of Hitler as war lord was his own ideological preferences, which made him give the invasion of Britain a lower priority than destroying the Communist Soviet Union. As a result, Nazi Germany ended up fighting a war on two fronts. Finally, Hitler failed to develop a co-ordinated and global military strategy with his two principal allies: Italy and Japan. Indeed, Hitler took very little interest in the conflict in the Mediterranean, the Battle of the Atlantic and the Pacific War.

The successful Nazi Blitzkrieg, 1939–40

The defeat of Poland

The original participants in the Second World War numbered just four (Germany, Poland, France and Britain). As Britain and France sat on the defensive in the west, giving no help whatsoever to Poland, there were only two active military participants in the first struggle of the war: Germany and Poland. The German army intended to achieve a swift victory over Poland. To complete the task, Germany deployed 55 divisions; 16 were fully mechanised (at a time when horses were still used) and a further six were the fearsome panzer divisions, consisting of mobile tank units. The German army used Blitzkrieg tactics – a new type of terrifying lightning warfare, consisting of rapid assaults by tanks, motorised infantry and aircraft. These swift-movement tactics achieved rapid advances against a Polish army with 30 poorly equipped divisions, attempting a static defence, with few tanks and 600 front-line aircraft. In less than a week, most of the Polish army units were surrounded. On 27 September 1939, Warsaw surrendered, having been virtually bombed to the ground by the screeching Stuka dive bombers. In less than a month, Nazi Germany had comprehensively defeated the Polish army. As a reward for signing the Nazi–Soviet pact, the Soviet Union occupied Latvia, Lithuania and Estonia. More surprisingly, the Soviet Union attacked Finland on 30 November 1939, but subzero temperatures and difficult operational conditions enabled the Finnish army to hold out until 12 March 1940.

The Phoney War

The speed of the Nazi victory over Poland gave Hitler enormous military confidence. He wanted a swift assault on western Europe, but the German attack in the west, originally set by Hitler for 12 November 1939, was postponed 29 times owing to planning, weather and transport difficulties. The British press described the lack of fighting in western Europe during the winter of 1939–40 as the 'Phoney War'. On 6 October 1941, Hitler said in a speech to the Reichstag: 'Why should this war in the west be fought? For Poland? Poland of the Versailles Treaty will never rise again.'[4] These 'peace' proposals to Britain and France by Hitler were rejected.

Denmark and Norway fall to Hitler, 1940

In the early months of 1940, pressure mounted on Britain and France to end what the British press were now calling the 'Sitzkrieg' on the western front. In March 1940, the British and French governments decided to try to halt German supplies of iron ore from Sweden, which passed through the Norwegian sea port of Narvik. But Hitler decided to thwart the Anglo-French plan by seizing Denmark and Norway. The German attack on Denmark (9 April 1940) ended in a German victory in a matter of hours. In Norway, the German army met stiff resistance from the Norwegian army, supported by British and French forces. German tanks were less decisive in the Norwegian campaign, but the overwhelming air superiority of the Luftwaffe (the German air-force) proved vital to the eventual German victory, which was completed on 10 June 1940. The Anglo-French defeat in Norway led to the fall of Neville Chamberlain and his replacement by Winston Churchill as British Prime Minister.

The Nazi victory in western Europe, 1940

The German offensive in western Europe finally began on 10 May 1940. It is often thought the German army enjoyed overwhelming military superiority over the western allies (Britain, France, Belgium and Holland). But this is not true. The Germans deployed 134 divisions against a roughly equal number of combined allied forces.[5] The British and French had 3,200 tanks against 2,500 German ones. It was in the air where the Germans were vastly superior, with 3,000 aircraft facing a combined allied total of 1,762.

The crucial difference between the sides was not in numbers or equipment, but in planning and tactics. French and British army commanders expected the main thrust of the German attack to come through Holland and Belgium.[6] Most leading German army commanders did support such an assault. But Hitler thought an attack on Belgium and Holland was too predictable. Von Manstein, the most brilliant German general, came up with a bolder plan in which the attack on Belgium and Holland would act as a diversion to draw the bulk of the allied forces away from the major Blitzkrieg assault, which was to be directed through the heavily wooded Ardennes region. This bold plan, if successful, would allow the German army to drive, virtually unimpeded, through French territory to the Channel coast, thereby cutting off the Anglo-French forces, which were expected to rush into Belgium to meet what they thought was the location of the major German thrust. Hitler decided to adopt von Manstein's plan.

It was the German tactical plan which really made the difference. The western allies were confused by the German tactics. The thrust through the Ardennes worked perfectly. The British expeditionary force and large numbers of French troops became trapped in a corridor by advancing German troops. The Germans won in less than five weeks, without ever facing a major counterattack from the western allies. Holland was captured on 15 May 1940; Belgium fell to the German army on 28 May 1940. The expeditionary force literally gave up, left their equipment behind and dashed to the coastal town of Dunkirk in the hope of escape. Between 27 May and 4 June 1940, 338,226 troops, including 140,000 French soldiers, were evacuated back to Britain. Hitler showed no willingness to prevent this vast exodus: 'It is always good to let a broken army return home to show the civilian population what a beating they have had.'[7]

The situation of the French army was now hopeless. On 10 June 1940, Mussolini finally decided to join the war on the side of Nazi Germany. Mussolini's decision extended the European war to the Mediterranean and North Africa. Ultimately, Italy proved a liability to Hitler as he constantly had to divert military resources to bolster Italian military weakness. On 14 June 1940, German troops entered Paris. On 16 June 1940, Paul Reynaud, the French leader, was replaced by Marshal Henri Philippe Pétain, who immediately sought an armistice. The armistice between Germany and France was signed on 22 June 1940 in the very same railway carriage at Compiègne where the Germans had signed the armistice in 1918. Under the terms of the armistice, all northern France, including Paris, and the Atlantic coast were occupied by German troops, while the south and south-east were granted partial independence, under Marshal Pétain's government based at the spa town of Vichy.[8]

The Battle of Britain, 1940

After the fall of France, Hitler hoped the British government would 'see it my way' and finally agree to accept German hegemony in Europe. In Hitler's view the British and the German people 'belong together racially and traditionally – this is and always has been my aim, even if our generals cannot grasp it'.[9] But Churchill promised that if Germany attempted an invasion, the British people would 'fight them on the beaches, fight them on the landing grounds, we shall fight them in the streets, we shall fight them on the hills; we shall never surrender'.[10] It was clear the British would fight on alone in what seemed a hopeless struggle against Nazi Germany.

The refusal of the British government to come to peace terms forced a reluctant Hitler to issue a directive on 16 July 1940 for the invasion of the British Isles (code-named Operation Sealion). From the beginning, Hitler had no enthusiasm for the project. Field Marshal Karl von Rundstedt, nominally in charge of the proposed invasion, later claimed the plan was 'nonsense' because adequate ships were not available and also because Hitler 'never really wanted to invade England'.[11] For Operation Sealion to have any chance of success, it was clear the Luftwaffe would need to establish overwhelming air superiority over the British coast.

The Battle of Britain in 1940, therefore, was solely an air war, fought between a comparatively small number of pilots on both sides. Of course, the Luftwaffe had a massive numerical superiority in aircraft, but the Germans chose not to engage their entire air-force with Britain. The British, however, had a number of important technological advantages over the Luftwaffe including: a centrally controlled fighter command centre; a chain of radar stations, which could track the path of incoming German aircraft; the Enigma Codebreaker, smuggled to Britain by exiled Polish airmen in 1939, which allowed the British to monitor German secret instructions; and, finally, British planes had ground-to-air radio communications.

The most crucial phase of the Battle of Britain was between 12 August and 15 September 1940. Between 23 August and 6 September 1940, the Royal Air Force (RAF) lost 466 fighters (either destroyed or severely damaged), while the

Luftwaffe suffered a loss of 385 aircraft. On 7 September 1940, the Luftwaffe switched its attack from bombing coastal shipping and RAF air bases, towards engaging in massive bomb attacks on London. These attacks inflicted great damage and many casualties, but caused the Germans to lose more aircraft. More importantly, the Luftwaffe attacks on London eased the pressure on the beleaguered RAF bases. On 15 September 1940, the Luftwaffe mounted a massive daylight attack on London, but a total of 60 German aircraft were shot down, compared with 26 British losses. This proved a decisive turning point. It showed the Luftwaffe could not gain air superiority in daylight over Britain. On 17 September 1940, Hitler postponed Operation Sealion, and the plan was never revived. Between 10 July 1940 and 31 October 1940, the Luftwaffe lost 1,389 aircraft, compared with a total loss of 792 on the British side.[12] Bomb attacks on Britain during the Second World War caused 51,509 deaths, but did not disrupt wartime production.

Hitler decides to attack the Soviet Union

Hitler now turned his attention towards the invasion of the Soviet Union. The Nazi–Soviet pact had always been viewed by Hitler as a temporary arrangement. In 1939, for example, Hitler told a League of Nations official: 'Everything that I undertake is directed against Russia. If those in the west are too stupid, and too blind to understand this, then I shall be forced to come to an understanding with the Russians to beat the west, and then, after its defeat, turn with all my concerted force against the Soviet Union.'[13] These views roughly coincide with Hitler's actions during the early stages of the Second World War.

The decision to attack the Soviet Union, even though it forced Nazi Germany to fight on two fronts, was taken more because it fitted in with Hitler's own territorial and ideological aims rather than for sound strategic reasons. It made more sense to concentrate on weakening the British position in the Mediterranean and the Middle East and stepping up U-boat (submarine) attacks on British shipping. Hitler did toy with this strategy, but eventually decided to launch the attack on the Soviet Union instead. On 18 December 1940, Hitler issued the order for the attack on the Soviet Union (code-named 'Operation Barbarossa'), with 1 May 1941 set as the earliest possible date for the opening of the campaign. Hitler planned the invasion of the Soviet Union on the assumption it would be completed in five months.

Yet the Soviet Union was, in Churchill's memorable phrase, 'a mystery wrapped up in an enigma'.[14] Very little was known about Stalin's regime, although a great deal of highly prejudiced opinion poured scorn on every aspect of it. Everyone knew Stalin had modernised industry in the Soviet Union, but no one could predict what impact this would have on Soviet military prowess. Most military experts (outside the Soviet Union) had a very low opinion of the numerically strong Red Army. In retrospect, it can be seen that much of what was written about the Soviet Union during the inter-war years was extremely prejudiced and misleading.

Diversion in the Balkans and North Africa

Meanwhile, Mussolini's decision to expand Italian territory in the Balkans and North Africa created a crisis for the Axis powers (Germany, Italy and Japan). On 28 October 1940, Italy attacked Greece, but did not gain a victory. In North Africa, Mussolini's attempt to capture territory at the expense of the British Empire also foundered. By the spring of 1940, Hitler decided to send troops to the Balkans and North Africa to restore the position of the Axis powers there. It has been claimed that clearing up the awkward situation in the Balkans forced Hitler to delay Operation Barbarossa from 15 May to 22 June 1941. Yet there is no evidence that a final date for the attack on the Soviet Union had been fixed. The date finally selected for Barbarossa was exactly the same as that of Napoleon's ill-fated attack on Russia in 1812. Given Hitler's great sense of history, it seems likely that 22 June was the date he always had in mind. In any case, the limited number of troops Hitler sent to the Balkans and North Africa in April 1940 were not diverted from the massive forces being assembled to attack the Soviet Union. It is probably worth adding that the German high command thought the Soviet Union would capitulate in weeks, not months.

German military action in the Balkans was prompted by the overthrow of a pro-Nazi government in Yugoslavia. On 6 April 1940, German troops attacked Yugoslavia, gaining victory in less than a week. On 9 April 1940, the Greek army, which had held the Italian army for six months, with the aid of 53,000 British troops, was overwhelmed by the German army in a matter of days. At the end of April, Germany was also dominant in the Balkans. To restore the Italian position in North Africa, Hitler sent a single armoured division – with limited air support – in March 1940 (under the command of General Erwin Rommel), which quickly recaptured Italian territory lost to the British and then forced the British army into headlong retreat in North Africa. On 27 May 1940, a small group of German paratroopers forced the British to surrender the island of Crete. By the end of May 1941, Germany had gained another series of dazzling military victories.

The bizarre flight of Rudolf Hess

The most bizarre incident to occur before the German attack on the Soviet Union occurred on 10 May 1941, when Rudolf Hess, Hitler's deputy, apparently acting on his own initiative, flew to Scotland in an eccentric attempt to persuade Britain to come to a peace settlement. Hess explained to the Duke of Hamilton that Hitler wanted a peace settlement with Britain. Hitler denied any knowledge of the flight of Hess and was greatly embarrassed by the incident. Yet the motive of the visit – to gain a pact with Britain in order to isolate the Soviet Union – certainly fitted in with Hitler's usual diplomatic pattern before a major military attack. Hess probably acted on his own initiative, but his attempt to conclude an Anglo-German pact was quite plainly a serious topic on the minds of the Nazi leadership in the weeks leading up to Operation Barbarossa.[15] The British press treated the flight of Hess as a huge joke. The poet A. P. Herbert summed up the general British view of Hess: 'He is insane. / He is a dove of peace. / He is a messiah. / He is Hitler's niece.'[16] Hess was hauled off to the Tower of London to become the most famous British prisoner of the Second World War.

Operation Barbarossa: the first phase, 22 June–December 1941

The German attack on the Soviet Union began at 3.30 a.m. on the morning of 22 June 1941. The attack stretched across a broad front of 1,500 miles from the Arctic Ocean to the Black Sea (see Map 1). The horrific battles between Nazi Germany and the Soviet Union unquestionably decided the outcome of the Second World War. Hitler told his generals that the struggle in the Soviet Union would be a war of racial purification (see Chapter 7) and utter destruction. At 6 a.m. on the morning of the attack, the people of Germany awoke to hear a radio message from the Nazi dictator: 'People of Germany! National Socialists! The hour has come . . . the fate and future of the German Reich is in the hands of our soldiers.'[17] Once the German attack on the Soviet Union was under way, Hitler was 'spiritually relieved', as he always saw the Nazi–Soviet pact as 'irksome' and a break with 'my whole origin and concepts'. Hitler was supremely confident of a swift victory: 'We only have to kick in the door and the whole rotten structure will come crashing down.'[18] The Nazi dictator moved from Berlin to his new military headquarters: a gloomy barracks, situated in a forest region, seven miles outside Rastenburg, East Prussia, known as *die Wolfsschanze* ('the Wolf's Lair'). Here Hitler was to remain for most of the remainder of the Second World War.

The Germans committed 153 divisions (3 million troops), supported by 18 Finnish divisions, 16 from Romania and 3 each from Italy and Slovakia during the initial phase of the attack. The Soviet Red Army had 150 poorly equipped divisions (2.8 million troops) located in the border areas and another 133 divisions (2 million troops) far away from the front line. The Germans deployed 3,350 modern tanks and 2,510 aircraft against 1,800 Russian tanks and 6,500 aircraft. For the purposes of the attack, the German army was divided into three separate armies:

1 Army Group North, consisting of 6 panzer and 26 infantry divisions, drove north-east, quickly capturing the Baltic states, and headed for Leningrad;
2 Army Group Centre, with 15 panzer units and 35 infantry divisions, rapidly advanced 450 miles, capturing Minsk and Smolensk on the way, eventually getting to within 30 miles of Moscow in late November 1941;
3 Army Group South, which had 8 tank units and 33 German infantry divisions supplemented by 14 Romanian divisions, advanced south-eastwards towards the Crimea, the Ukraine, eventually hoping to seize the oil fields in the Caucasus and Stalingrad – a great industrial centre situated on the Volga River.

In the first three months of Operation Barbarossa, 2.8 million Soviet troops were killed, wounded or captured. On 3 October 1941, Hitler was so confident of victory he informed the German people: 'the enemy in the east has been struck down and will never rise again'. Yet the Red Army, though terribly assaulted, was

SWEDEN

NORWAY

Murmansk

Archangel

USSR

URAL MOUNTAINS

Helsinki

Leningrad

Riga

Moscow

BALTIC SEA

Rastenburg

Smolensk

Berlin

Warsaw

Minsk

Prague

Kursk
Kharkov

R. Volga

Stalingrad

R. Oder

Kiev

R. Donets

Vienna

Budapest

R. Dnieper

R. Dniester

UKRAINE

Rostov

GERMAN-DOMINATED
EUROPE

Bucharest

CRIMEA

CASPIAN SEA

Belgrade

BLACK SEA

CAUCASUS
MOUNTAINS

Sofia

TURKEY

IRAN

MEDITERRANEAN SEA

N

Eastern frontier of German-dominated
territory at start of attack on the USSR,
22 June 1941

Front line on 5 December 1941

| 0 | 200 | 400 | 600 km |
| 0 | | 200 | 400 miles |

Map 1. The attack on the Soviet Union, 1941.

very far from defeated. In most of the previous battles of the Second World War, the German army had turned early success into swift victory, thus avoiding being dragged into a stamina-sapping struggle. In the Soviet campaign, the German army faced supremely heroic soldiers, who took a terrible battering in 1941, got up off the floor and regrouped and re-equipped to bring about the most remarkable come-back of any army in military history. According to a leading German general: 'the conduct of the Russian troops was in stark contrast to the behaviour of the Poles and the Western Allies in defeat. Even when encircled the Russians stood their ground and fought'.[19] General Halder wrote in his diary in August 1941: 'we underestimated the strength of the Russian colossus'.[20]

By September, Operation Barbarossa had slowed down. The halt in the attack provoked a debate between Hitler and his generals. The generals favoured an all-out push towards Moscow, but Hitler decided this could wait until Leningrad and the important oil fields in the south were captured. It was only in early September 1941, probably too late in the year, that Hitler changed his mind and ordered a push towards Moscow. By late November 1941, Germany had still not captured the city.

On 6 December 1941, the Red Army defending Moscow, under the inspired command of General Georgi Zhukov, the most brilliant military commander in the Second World War, launched the most effective counterattack the German army had faced in the Second World War. The German armed forces were forced into a 75-mile retreat from Moscow. In the south, the Red Army recaptured Rostov, pushing back the German advance by 50 miles. Thus, even before the USA entered the war on 7 December 1941, following Japan's surprise attack on Pearl Harbor, the seemingly unstoppable march of the German army in Europe had been halted. Indeed, the Soviet counterattack which saved Moscow in 1941 sent panic through the now exhausted German army, which very nearly collapsed under the strain in the cold and depressing winter of 1941–42. It was only Hitler's order on 18 December 1941 for German troops to stand and hold their positions which helped to stabilise the situation.

The German campaign in the Soviet Union, 1942–43

In the early months of 1942, Hitler realised the original plan to attack the Soviet Union across a wide front had failed. He decided to order a retreat by Army Group Centre to more defensible lines, approximately 100 miles away from Moscow. The original plan to attack all along the battle line with equal momentum was now abandoned. In any case, Germany now lacked the military resources to attack on three fronts simultaneously. Hitler put the blame for the failure to achieve a swift victory on his generals: he sacked 35 of them during the winter of 1941–42.

Hitler decided the main aim of the German campaign in the Soviet Union for 1942 would be a summer offensive in the south, with two aims: to conquer the Caucasus oil fields; and to capture Stalingrad. Many of Hitler's generals doubted whether attempting two objectives simultaneously, over 300 miles apart, was a

Map 2. Europe under Nazi influence, 1942.

sensible idea, but Hitler had his way. In the offensive, the German army fielded 68 divisions, supported by 27 Romanian and 13 Bulgarian divisions.

The second major German offensive against the Red Army began on 28 June 1942 and was initially successful. On 23 July 1942, the Germans captured Rostov. But Hitler now made a major military blunder. He decided to capture Stalingrad before first seizing the oil fields in the Caucasus, which appeared well within reach. At the end of August 1942, the German 6th Army – consisting of 20 German and 2 Romanian divisions, led by General Friedrich von Paulus, reached the Volga, just north of Stalingrad.

The major turning point: the Battle of Stalingrad, 1942–43

In 1942, Stalingrad was a major port and industrial city, located on the west bank of the River Volga; it spanned 25 miles along the river and was three miles wide inland. The city was defended by the 62nd Soviet Army, under the brilliant command of General Chuikov. His troops prepared to defend Stalingrad street by street. Chuikov believed that German Blitzkrieg tactics, originally startling and bewildering to their opponents, had now become inflexible and predictable. The German infantry went into battle only after the tanks had caused havoc. The tanks went into battle only after the Luftwaffe had dropped its bombs. Chuikov realised that if he could draw the German soldiers into close fighting in the city, the tanks and the Luftwaffe would be of no use and the preferred German tactic of Blitzkrieg would be nullified. Once Chuikov had drawn the German 6th Army into Stalingrad, a large offensive could then be mounted by the Red Army, with the aim of surrounding Stalingrad and cutting off the 6th Army from its sources of supply. The plan of the Red Army at Stalingrad worked brilliantly. Chuikov did lure the 6th Army into Stalingrad on 19 August 1942, where it was forced to fight a bitter struggle street by street.

On 19 November 1942, the Red Army outside the city, commanded by Zhukov, launched a massive counteroffensive to the north and south of Stalingrad. On 22 November 1942, Zhukov took 65,000 Romanian troops prisoner, decimated a whole Italian army and surrounded the German 6th Army at Stalingrad under the command of von Paulus. For the first time, the German army had been completely outmanoeuvred by the superior tactics of the enemy. Worse was to follow. On 16 December 1942, the Red Army launched a second major offensive in the south, which sent the German army into a hasty retreat in the Caucasus.

The situation of the German army in Stalingrad was now hopeless. On 27 December 1942, General Kurt Zeitzler advised Hitler to abandon the campaign in the Caucasus completely or face 'another Stalingrad'. Hitler reluctantly agreed to this request, but he refused to allow the 6th Army at Stalingrad to retreat or surrender. On 30 January 1943, ironically the tenth anniversary of Hitler coming to power, von Paulus informed the Nazi leader, 'collapse could not be delayed'. The next day, Hitler promoted von Paulus to the rank of field marshal, in the full knowledge that no German soldier of that rank had ever been taken prisoner. On 2 February 1943, von Paulus, along with 24 other German generals, did surrender, along with 91,000 beleaguered, starving, frost-bitten and utterly beaten German troops. The most decisive battle of the Second World War had been won by the Red Army. The aura of German military invincibility was shattered. There is little doubt that the victory of the Red Army at Stalingrad was the most crucial turning point in the Second World War.

Military defeats for the Axis powers, 1942–44

During 1942–43, Germany and Italy suffered many other major defeats in North Africa, the Atlantic and the Mediterranean theatres of war. In October 1942, the British 8th Army, under General Bernard Montgomery, defeated General Erwin Rommel's inadequately supplied Afrika Korps at el Alamein. This was followed in November 1942 by major Anglo-American landings in North Africa. By early May 1943, Anglo-American troops had cleared German and Italian forces out of North Africa.

In April 1943, the German navy conceded defeat in the Battle of the Atlantic by withdrawing submarines back to base. Anglo-American ships now enjoyed complete control of the sea lanes, thus paving the way to preparations for the Anglo-American assault on western Europe, code-named D-Day, in June 1944. By the summer of 1943, the 'Big Three' allied leaders – Stalin (Soviet Union), Roosevelt (USA) and Churchill (Britain) – were extremely confident of ultimate victory and demanded 'unconditional surrender' from the Axis powers.

In July 1943, 180,000 Anglo-American troops landed in Sicily. On 25 July 1943, Mussolini fell from power, but was sprung from jail in a daring raid by German troops to set up the German puppet Salò Republic in northern Italy. On 8 September 1943, the new democratic Italian government announced an armistice with the allies. When British and US troops invaded Italy, they met little resistance in the south, but did face stiff German resistance in the north. The German army in northern Italy went on the defensive and offered prolonged resistance to Anglo-American troops. Rome was not taken by the allies until 5 June 1944. The allies gained victory only in the spring of 1945.

In the Asian-Pacific conflict, Japan, which had enjoyed early success in 1941–42, was now facing a massive US counteroffensive in 1942–43, which was gradually giving the USA naval and air superiority in the Pacific region.

The failure of 'Operation Citadel': the Red Army gains the upper hand

The military situation facing Germany in 1943 was extremely serious. There were strong arguments put forward by the German high command to Hitler for the adoption of a defensive strategy on the eastern front. But Hitler decided to launch a fresh offensive on 21 February 1943. The chief aim of the third major German offensive in the Soviet Union was to recapture the territory lost in the Russian counteroffensive in the south in the winter of 1942–43. On 19 March 1943, the Germans captured Belgorod, but the Red Army managed to create a bulge in the line of the German advance at Kursk, a vital communications centre in the south.

Hitler decided to use his panzer divisions to make a major assault on the Red Army at Kursk (the operation was code-named 'Citadel'). Hitler told his generals: 'The victory at Kursk must shine like a beacon to the world.'[21] On 4 July 1943, the German army launched the largest tank assault of the war at Kursk, involving the deployment of 3,000 vehicles. The Germans faced over 4,000 modern tanks of the Red Army. In less than a week, the Red Army, commanded by Zhukov once again, halted the massive German tank attack on Kursk, destroying over 1,500 German tanks and over 1,000 German planes. To prevent the complete destruction of all German panzer units, Hitler ordered a hasty retreat. The failure of Operation Citadel was another decisive German defeat. The Red Army had met the German Blitzkrieg head on and repulsed it, without much difficulty.

The Red Army drives Germany back, 1943–44

The pattern of the war on the eastern front from mid-1943 until the end of the war in 1945 was now firmly set: repeated Soviet offensives all along the wide front, punctuated only by stubborn German resistance, which was eventually broken. Hitler now believed Germany would not win against the Soviet Union and he increasingly blamed his generals for the continuing defeats. Confidence within the Red Army was now sky high. With new equipment – modern tanks, US-made jeeps, trucks, and devastating artillery weapons – the Red Army by mid-1943 was a formidable fighting unit, which could actually move and manoeuvre more quickly than the retreating and increasingly less well equipped German army. The Red Army pushed the German army backward and backward, out of the Soviet Union, and eventually all the way back to Berlin. As Goebbels wrote in his diary in August 1943: 'It is a curious thing, that although every individual soldier returning from the Eastern Front considers himself superior to the Bolshevik soldier, we are still retreating and retreating.'[22]

For the remainder of 1943, the Red Army launched a series of bold counter-offensives. In the south, the Red Army drove the Germans back 150 miles towards Poland. The Red Army was also pushing the Germans back in central and northern Russia. The winter of 1943–44 should have provided some hope to the Germans: it was very mild, dry and warm. Yet it was the Red Army which took the initiative in a series of bold offensives. It was now clear that Germany would lose the war on the eastern front. The only remaining question was how long it would take.

The attack in western Europe

D-Day, 6 June 1944

The military situation of Nazi Germany grew even more desperate on 6 June 1944 ('D-Day'), when the much-awaited cross-Channel Anglo-American invasion of western Europe, commanded by US General Dwight D. Eisenhower, finally began with mass landings at Normandy. The attack on western Europe (code-named 'Operation Overlord') was the largest amphibious assault in military and naval history. The German army defended the assault with 58 poorly equipped divisions. The western allies had 37 well-equipped and fresh divisions and, once they consolidated their hold on the Channel ports, landed 40 more divisions. The major advantages of the allies were: modern tanks, overwhelming air superiority and seemingly unlimited supplies of manpower and equipment.

Once the allies had managed to consolidate their position, the fate of the defending German forces was sealed. The allies quickly liberated Belgium and Luxembourg and were racing northwards through France towards the German border on the Rhine. On 24 August 1944, French and American troops marched into Paris. On 3 September 1944, the British army, under Montgomery, captured Brussels. The next day the key port of Antwerp was under allied control. The only major hitch to the allied advance in the first three months after the D-Day landing occurred on 17 September 1944, when a small British force failed to capture an important bridge over the Rhine at Arnhem. The allies decided in the autumn of 1944 to pause along the Rhine, partly because of supply difficulties and partly because of stiff resistance along the German border.

Hitler's last offensive: the Ardennes, 1944–45

Hitler now decided to mount a last-ditch offensive at the Ardennes, in the hope this might turn the tide on the western front. The final German offensive (dubbed the 'Battle of the Bulge') began on 16 December 1944. The US army was initially taken by surprise, but with a combination of speedier tanks and overwhelming air superiority the German assault was held. On 3 January 1945, the allies launched a massive counterattack, which, by 16 January 1945, had pushed the German army right back to where it had started. Hitler's final gamble had failed. The US generals knew – by studying what had happened in the Soviet Union – that if the initial Blitzkrieg attack could be held, followed by a powerful counterattack, then the German army could be forced into a retreat. By the end of January 1945, as Anglo-American troops crossed the Rhine, most of west and southern Germany lay at their mercy.

The final assault on Nazi Germany, 1944–45

Meanwhile, the Red Army kept up its forward advance on the eastern front. A major Soviet offensive, planned to coincide with the D-Day landings, began on 22 June 1944. The date chosen by Stalin for this massive Red Army offensive was the third anniversary of Operation Barbarossa. The offensive inflicted the biggest territorial losses of the Second World War on the German army. It showed how much the initiative had passed to the Red Army. Hitler knew the attack was imminent. He ordered a massed static defence against it. The superiority of the Red Army made this impossible. By this stage, Soviet tanks outnumbered the Germans by a staggering ten to one and aircraft by eight to one. Within a fortnight, the three major German armies in the Soviet Union were smashed to pieces. At the end of August 1944, the Red Army drove the German army out of most of the Soviet territory it had previously occupied. By the end of September 1944, the Red Army had captured Bulgaria and Romania from the Nazis. By late November 1944, they had driven the Nazis out of Yugoslavia, surrounded Budapest, the capital of Hungary, and were on the border of Poland. Hitler now departed from the Wolf's Lair in East Prussia and returned to Germany to undertake the defence of Berlin.

The final Red Army offensive began on 12 January 1945. Zhukov led the final assault on Nazi Germany and in less than a fortnight had advanced to less than 100 miles outside Berlin. On 17 January 1945, Warsaw, the capital of Poland, was captured and the next day Budapest fell. On 20 January 1945, the Red Army entered East Prussia. German troops evacuated Tannenberg; they dug up the remains of President Hindenburg and transported them back to Berlin. The Red Army next captured the vital industrial area of Silesia, prompting Albert Speer, the Nazi Armaments Minister, to tell Hitler: 'The war is lost.'[23]

The last days of Hitler

By the end of March 1945, all German military resistance was completely broken. Anglo-American armies were on German soil. On 16 April 1945, Eisenhower captured Nuremberg, where Hitler had held his major Nazi rallies. On 18 April 1945, 325,000 German troops defending the Ruhr surrendered. Meanwhile, on the eastern front, the march of the Red Army was irresistible. On 11 April 1945, Vienna, capital of Hitler's 'beloved' Austria, was captured by Soviet troops. On 21 April 1945, Zhukov, who had prevented Hitler's armies capturing Moscow in 1941, and Stalingrad and Kursk in 1943, now brought the Red Army to the outskirts of Berlin.

In the last days of April 1945, Hitler was located in a bunker 50 feet beneath the Reich Chancellery in Berlin. He decided that rather than personally surrender to the allies, he would commit suicide. Hitler's decision to end his own life was no doubt reinforced by news of the execution of Mussolini and his lover Claretta Petacci on 28 April 1945, by Italian partisans near Lake Como. The bodies of Mussolini and his mistress, riddled with bullets, were taken from there to Milan, where they were hung upside down in a public display on the Plaza Loreto.

On 29 April 1945, Hitler married Eva Braun in the map room of the Führerbunker. Yet, even in the face of utter defeat, with sole responsibility for millions of deaths, Hitler expressed no regrets and no remorse. On the contrary, one of the final acts of his life was to write his last will and testament, in which he denied he wanted war in 1939, blaming it on those international statesmen who 'were either of Jewish descent or worked for Jewish interests'. He went on to place the major blame for the German military defeat on the 'treachery' of the officer class of the German army. To further emphasise his contempt for the army, he nominated Admiral Karl Doenitz as his successor.

On 30 April 1945, at 3.30 p.m., Hitler, accompanied by Eva Braun, went into their bedroom in the bunker. A few seconds later a single gun shot was heard by his personal staff waiting outside. Adolf Hitler had shot himself through the head, simultaneously biting on a cyanide capsule. Eva Braun had taken a cyanide capsule and died within seconds. Shortly afterwards, the bodies of Hitler and Eva Braun, wrapped in blankets, were carried upstairs and set on fire in the Chancellery garden.

The next day, Joseph Goebbels, who had stayed with the Nazi leader in the bunker at the end, also committed suicide, as did his wife, who also gave cyanide to all their six children. It is now known that the Red Army, which captured the bunker on the evening of 1 May 1945, got hold of Hitler's remains, but all that is now left are fragments of Hitler's skull, held in an archive in Moscow. On 7 May 1945, the German authorities signed the unconditional surrender which ended the Second World War and put an end to Nazi Germany.

The end of the Third Reich, 1945. German refugees in the devastated centre of Berlin with the remains of the Brandenburg Gate in the background.

Hitler at war, 1939–45

6.1 Hitler appeals to 'the reason of England' to end the war, July 1940

Mr. Churchill has just declared again that he wants war . . . I am quite aware of the fact that people will suffer incredible misery and misfortune from our impending response. Naturally this will not affect Mr. Churchill, for he will certainly be in Canada where the property and the children of the most important people who have an interest in the war have already been taken. But for millions of other people there will be great misery. And perhaps Mr. Churchill may believe me for once when I prophesy the following: A great empire will be destroyed. A world empire that I never intended to destroy or damage. But it is clear to me the continuation of this struggle will end with the complete destruction of one of the two opponents. Mr. Churchill may believe this will be Germany. I know it will be England. At this hour I feel compelled by conscience once more to appeal to reason in England. I believe I am in a position to do this because I am not the vanquished begging favours. As a victor, I am speaking in the name of reason. I can see no reason why this war should go on.

Source: Raoul de Roussy de Sales (ed.), *Adolf Hitler: my new order*, New York, 1941, pp. 809, 838

6.2 Hitler explains to Mussolini his decision to attack the Soviet Union, June 1941

Since I struggled through to this decision, I again feel spiritually free. The partnership with the Soviet Union in spite of the complete sincerity of the efforts to bring about a final conciliation, was nevertheless often very irksome to me, for in some way or other it seemed to me to break with my whole origin, my concepts, and my former obligations. I am happy to be relieved of these mental agonies.

Source: *Documents on German foreign policy*, series D, vol. 12, p. 1066

6.3 A German general expresses concerns about 'the Russian colossus', August 1941

The whole situation makes it increasingly plain that we have underestimated the Russian colossus, who consistently prepared for war with that utterly ruthless determination so characteristic of Totalitarian States. This applies to organizational and economic resources as well as to the communication system and, most of all, to the strictly military potential. At the outset of the war we reckoned with about 200 enemy divisions. Now we have counted 360. These divisions are not armed and equipped to our standards, and their tactical leadership is often poor. But there they are, and if we smash a dozen of them, the Russians simply put up another dozen. The time factor favours them, as they are near their own resources, whereas we are moving farther and farther away from ours.

Source: J. Noakes and G. Pridham (eds.), *Nazism 1919–1945. A documentary reader, Vol. 3: Foreign policy, war and racial extermination*, Exeter, 1988, p. 820

6.4 Hitler is confident of victory at Stalingrad, November 1942

What our soldiers have achieved [during the attack on the Soviet Union] in terms of speed is tremendous. And what has been achieved this year is enormous and historically unprecedented. The fact that I don't do things the way other people want – well, I consider what the others like to think and then I do things differently on principle. So Mr. Stalin expected us to attack in the centre – I had no intention of attacking in the centre. Not because Mr. Stalin may have believed I wanted to, but because I was not interested. I wanted to get to the Volga at a certain point near a certain town. As it happens, its name is that of Stalin himself. But please do not think I marched there for that reason – it could be called something quite different – I did so because it is a very important place. Thirty million tons of transport can be cut off there, including nearly nine million tons of oil. All the wheat from the vast Ukraine and the Kuban area converges there to be transported north . . . I wanted to take it and, you know, we are being modest, for we have got it! There are only a few small places left not captured.

Source: M. Domarus (ed.), *Hitler. Reden 1932–1945*, Wiesbaden, 1973, pp. 1937–38

6.5 A Red Army general in Stalingrad feels confident of defeating the German army

The enemy stuck to the same pattern in his tactics. His infantry went into an attack wholeheartedly only when tanks had already reached the target. The tanks, however, normally went into the attack only when the Luftwaffe was already over the heads of our troops. One only had to break this sequence for an enemy attack to stop and his units to turn back . . . The Germans could not stand close fighting; they opened up with their automatic weapons from well over half a mile away, when their bullets could not cover half the distance. They fired simply to keep up their morale. They could not bear us to come close to them when we counter-attacked. Some threw themselves to the ground, and often retreated.

Source: V. I. Chuikov, *The beginning of the road*, London, 1963, pp. 71–72

6.6 Hitler predicts the allied coalition will fall apart, April 1944

The Führer had spent a lot of time reading history recently and had noted that most coalitions hardly lasted for five years. The fact that our allies remained loyal to us, despite the long period of war, was only because Fascism ruled Italy and because the Hungarians, Romanians and Finns were bound to us by the Russian threat. Our enemies' coalition was unnatural. It involved two different worlds. One could rather imagine a German–Russian coalition than one between the egotistical capitalism of England and America and egotistical Bolshevism or anti capitalism . . . In addition, there was the conflict between England and America. America was quietly, and without a fuss about it plundering England on the basis of a system of pledges . . . The important thing was to hold on stubbornly, since the front of our opponents must break down one day.

Source: J. Noakes and G. Pridham (eds.), *Nazism 1919–1945. A documentary reader, Vol. 3: Foreign policy, war and racial extermination*, Exeter, 1988, pp. 868–69

6.7 Hitler argues that Germany was too 'weak' to win the war, March 1945

If the war is lost, the nation will also perish. This fate is inevitable. There is no necessity to take into consideration the basis which the people will need to continue a most primitive existence . . . this nation will have proved to be the weaker one and the future will belong to the stronger eastern nation [the Soviet Union]. Besides, those who remain after the battle are only inferior ones, for the good ones have been killed.

Source: W. Shirer, *The rise and fall of the Third Reich*, London, 1960, p. 1311

6.8 'No regrets': Hitler's last will and testament, April 1945

It is untrue that I or anybody in Germany wanted war in 1939. It was wanted and provoked by those international statesmen who were either of Jewish descent or worked for Jewish interests. I have made too many offers for the limitation and control of armaments. Which posterity will not for all time be able to disregard, for responsibility for the outbreak of this war to be placed on me. Further, I never wished that after the appalling First World War, there would be a second one against either England or America. Centuries will go by, but from the ruins of our towns and monuments the hatred of those ultimately responsible will always grow anew. They are the people whom we have to thank for all this: international Jewry and its helpers.

Source: W. Shirer, *The rise and fall of the Third Reich*, London, 1960, p. 1335

Document case-study questions

1 What is the purpose of Hitler's comments in 6.1?

2 What conclusion can be drawn about Hitler's attitude towards the Nazi–Soviet pact from 6.2?

3 How useful is 6.3 for a historian constructing a military history of the German campaign against the Soviet Union during the Second World War?

4 Suggest the reasons why Hitler views the capture of Stalingrad as so crucial for the German campaign in the Soviet Union.

5 What conclusions about the military skill of Red Army generals can be drawn from 6.5?

6 What does 6.6 tell us about Hitler's view of the likely course of the war in 1944?

7 Explain why Hitler's comments in 6.7 might be useful to a historian of Nazi ideology.

8 Do you find Hitler's comments on the outbreak of the war in 1939 as expressed in 6.8 in any way convincing?

Notes and references

1 E. von Manstein, *Lost victories*, London, 1958, pp. 274–76.

2 S. Lee, *The European dictatorships*, London, 1987, pp. 219–20.

3 A. Bullock, *Hitler: a study in tyranny*, revised edn, London, 1964, p. 674.

4 J. Toland, *Adolf Hitler*, New York, 1976, p. 801.

5 The western allies fielded the following number of divisions: French, 94; British, 10; Belgian, 22; Dutch, 8.

6 The view that Germany would attack Belgium and Holland was based on what had happened in the initial stages of the First World War.

7 Toland, *Hitler*, p. 836.

8 In 1943, the German army occupied the remainder of France and the French government at Vichy openly collaborated with their Nazi rulers.

9 Toland, *Hitler*, p. 836.

10 W. Shirer, *The rise and fall of the Third Reich*, London, 1960, p. 885.

11 *Ibid.*, p. 912.

12 In 1940, Britain produced 9,924 new aircraft, compared with the German total of 8,070.

13 I. Kershaw, *The Nazi Dictatorship. Problems and perspectives of interpretation*, 3rd edn, London, 1993, p. 125.

14 This quote is attributed to Winston Churchill.

15 The campaign was called Barbarossa (Red Beard) after Frederick I, the Holy Roman Emperor who marched east in 1190 to capture the Holy Land.

16 Toland, *Hitler*, p. 911.

17 *Ibid.*, p. 921.

18 *Ibid.*, p. 924.

19 Shirer, *Third Reich*, p. 1021.

20 *Ibid.*

21 M. Arnold Foster, *The world at war*, London, 1973, p. 169.

22 M. Gilbert, *Second World War*, London, 1989, p. 463.

23 Shirer, *Third Reich*, p. 1303.

7 Mass murder under Nazi rule

The most horrendous aspect of the history of Nazi Germany is the systematic mass murder carried out by the regime. At least 13 million people were killed in this way. The most prominent victims of this organised programme of extermination were the Jews of Europe. The term Holocaust (meaning burnt sacrifice/catastrophe) is often used to describe the killing of Jewish people under Nazi rule, while the term genocide (meaning systematic/state-organised killing) is a broader term which covers the many examples of organised death undertaken by the Nazi regime, including the murder of Jews. The Holocaust entailed the extermination of millions of Jews, many of whom were transported by train to purpose-built extermination centres, where they were gassed in shower rooms and their bodies burnt in adjacent crematoria.[1] And for what? In Hitler's words, for 'the maintenance of the purity of German blood'.[2]

The development of anti-Semitism

There was nothing new about Jews being subjected to persecution and murder in Europe. They were used to being treated as 'a problem' in need of a 'solution'. Ever since the triumph of Christianity in the fourth century AD, Jews were classed as the 'killers of Jesus Christ' and viewed as outsiders in most Christian countries. The Jews were a stateless people, always in a minority in every country in which they lived, often suffering from prejudice and persecution. In fifteenth-century Spain, there were mass killings of Jews. In late-nineteenth-century Russia there was a series of brutal mass killings (pogroms) of Jews. The Tsarist regime also confiscated Jewish property, confined Jews to ghettos and encouraged millions of Jews to emigrate. There were many other instances of anti-Jewish persecution throughout Europe, too numerous to mention. In response to these widely held feelings of anti-Semitism, Jewish religious leaders demanded their own state in Palestine, but this was not granted until 1948.[3]

Anti-Semitism in Germany

In Germany, anti-Semitism was long-standing. There were anti-Jewish outrages in Germany during the Reformation and the Peasants' War of the early sixteenth century. Martin Luther, the leading spirit in the German Reformation, was ferociously anti-Semitic. From 1807 to 1914, anti-Semitism in Germany continued, but it was accompanied by a gradual extension of civil rights. The most significant Jewish emancipation law in the early nineteenth century was the Prussian decree of 11 March 1812. Between 1869 and 1871, Jews were granted improved civil rights. As civil rights were extended, some Jews prospered, especially in the professions and business, but this did not end anti-Semitism.

Yet the German politicians who had supported equal rights for Jews were always out of tune with popular sentiment. Anti-Semitism remained widespread in Germany, in particular among white-collar workers, farmers, shopkeepers and independent artisans. A recent study of anti-Semitic writers in Germany between 1861 and 1895 has shown a substantial number proposing 'physical extermina-tion' as the best means of dealing with the *Judenfrage* ('Jewish question'). Many of these writers defined the Jews not as a religious group but as a unified 'race', subverting German society in order to improve their own political and economic position.

In 1914, popular anti-Semitism remained a fact of life in Germany. During the First World War, however, Jews were made eligible for promotion even to the officer rank in the Prussian army. After 1918, many right-wing nationalist groups called the Weimar Republic 'a Jewish Republic'. Anti-Jewish propaganda was prominent across the political spectrum in Germany from 1918 to 1933. Nazi propaganda made 'the Jews' a focus for every problem in Weimar Germany: inflation, unemployment and economic collapse.[4]

The twisted road to Auschwitz

Hitler expressed a violent hatred of Jews throughout his political career. At the very least, he wanted them 'eliminated' from German society. On coming to power in 1933, the exact means by which Hitler intended to translate his anti-Semitism into detailed policies was by no means clear. To be sure, a series of anti-Jewish measures was only to be expected, but it is worth emphasising that there was a 'twisted road to Auschwitz', not a direct route.[5] Hitler's anti-Semitism made the Holocaust a possibility – not an inevitability. The process towards the 'Final Solution' of the Jewish question evolved in stages, under the pressure of events, which could not be predicted in 1933. A great number of hurdles would have to be jumped before Hitler reached a point where he was able virtually to exterminate the European Jewish population.

Jewish discrimination in Nazi Germany, 1933–37

From 1933 to 1937, government legislation to withdraw civil rights from Jews was the chief weapon used by the Nazi regime. A great many Jews decided to leave Germany rather than face increased discrimination. In 1933, there were 525,000 Jews in Germany, but through emigration this figure had dwindled to 118,000 by 1938, and another 30,000 fled Germany when the war broke out.

In April 1933, the first of what eventually numbered 400 Nazi racial laws discriminating against Jews was put into effect. Jews were categorised as 'non-Aryans' and stripped of a great number of civil rights; this included exclusion from a university education, posts in government, the civil service, the army,

Hamburg, 1935. SA and SS members had themselves photographed with these two young people who were forced through the streets as 'discouraging examples'. The non-Jewish woman is carrying a sign reading 'I am the greatest swine in the area and only get involved with Jews.' The young man bears a sign reading 'As a Jew, I only take German girls up to my room.'

the media, farming and certain professions. A government-sponsored boycott of Jewish businesses took place on 1 April 1933, but it lasted only for one day. It was intended to be indefinite, but was abandoned because of diplomatic pressure from abroad and the cold economic calculation by Hitler that such a boycott would hamper German economic recovery. In the early years of the regime, Hitler appears 'moderate' on the Jewish question, often resisting, sometimes giving into demands by party activists for more radical anti-Semitic measures.

Even the enactment of the Nuremberg Laws on 15 September 1935, which formalised anti-Semitism into the Nazi state, was largely the result of party pressure from below. In the end, Hitler chose the most moderate version of four separate drafts of the Nuremberg Laws. These Laws defined a Jew as a person with any of the following characteristics: a Jewish parent; two or more Jewish grandparents; or any person who was a member of the Jewish religious community. It was also possible to be classed as a Jew through marriage to a Jew (this clause was eventually dropped), or by being the illegitimate offspring of someone with three or more Jewish grandparents. The first Nuremberg Law defined Reich citizenship as something which could be held only by a 'national of German or kindred blood'. Jews were defined as neither of German or kindred blood, but were not defined in exclusively genetic/racial terms. The second major Nuremberg Law, 'For the Protection of German Blood and German Honour', prohibited marriage between Germans and Jews and stripped Jews of all civil and political rights, defining them as 'non-citizens'. The Nuremberg Laws reveal the muddled racial ideas of the Nazi regime. Hitler had no clear idea what a Jew was, in either religious or genetic terms. However, the Nuremberg Laws did make Jews officially second-class citizens in Nazi Germany.

The growth of radical anti-Semitism, 1937–39

The turning point towards more open persecution of Jews took place from 1937 to 1939. Jews were driven out of certain towns, which declared themselves *judenfrei* ('Jew free'), or *judenrein* ('Jew pure'). Jewish people were banned from public swimming baths, sports grounds, parks, cafés, theatres and restaurants. The elimination of Jews from German social life did not provoke public outrage, or even disapproval. Jews also suffered from many isolated incidents of physical assault, most notably the forcible cutting of the beards and hair of orthodox Jews in public, and physical and verbal attacks. But most of these attacks were undertaken by Nazi activists at the local level, usually acting on their own initiative.

Throughout 1938 there was a further wave of anti-Jewish legislation, which banned Jewish doctors, salesmen, lawyers, vets and dentists, and virtually excluded Jews from German economic life. This state-led persecution culminated in the most openly violent act against the Jewish population within Nazi Germany before 1939: *Kristallnacht* ('Night of Broken Glass', on 9–10 November 1938), which saw 7,500 Jewish shops destroyed, 400 synagogues burnt down and over 90 Jews killed. It was Joseph Goebbels who initiated the pogrom, which was fully supported by Hitler and carried out by party activists, who had been itching to launch open violence against the Jews for years.

The trend of Nazi anti-Semitic policy from 1933 to 1939 was progressively radical, moving from legal discrimination to threats to the person, violence and a gradual deprivation of economic power. By 1939, Jews were 'eliminated' from the economic, political, legal, cultural and social life of Germany.[6] Yet the major aim of Nazi policy at this stage was not extermination but deportation.

The euthanasia programme, 1939–41

The euthanasia programme, which was not aimed at Jews, is the first example of organised mass murder undertaken by the Nazi regime.[7] This programme was directed towards those defined as 'racially inferior'. In August 1939, the T4 (euthanasia) programme was established, which ran until August 1941. It was designed as a programme of 'mercy killing' for the mentally ill and physically disabled. It was carried out in secret at six German mental hospitals (Bernburg, Brandenburg, Grafeneck, Hadamar, Hartheim and Sonnenstein). Yet the killing of over 100,000 of Germany's mentally ill and disabled children and adults was carried out without the consent of relatives or patients. This is a clear example of state-organised mass killing. After dabbling with lethal injections, the euthanasia centres chose gassing as their favoured method of killing. Shower rooms were transformed into gas chambers and postal vans were converted into mobile gas chambers. Relatives were told nothing about these deaths; false death certificates were issued and inquests timed so relatives could not attend. The T4 programme, which created many of the methods of killing which were later adopted in the Nazi death camps, reminds us that Nazi genocide encompassed a wide variety of victims whose lives became classed as worthless.

The persecution of the Jews, 1939–41

The anti-Semitic aspects of Nazi racial policy became transformed into a policy of extermination as Nazi control in Europe brought millions more Jews under German rule between 1939 and 1941. The defeat of Poland alone brought 2 million more Jews under Nazi rule. The conditions of war also allowed two key Nazi organisations – the SS (*Schutzstaffel*), led by Heinrich Himmler, and its security wing, the SD (*Sicherheitsdienst*), led by Reinhard Heydrich – to gain complete control over the process of carrying out racial policy in Nazi-occupied territories. The powerful influence of the SS and SD in implementing racial policy was increased by their amalgamation in September 1939 with the Gestapo and the criminal police to form the Reich Central Security Office (*Reichssicherheits-hauptamt* – RHSA). The RHSA was able to co-ordinate racial policy in a more centralised manner.

Poland was the first country to receive the full blast of Nazi racial policy. In Poland, the conditions for a Final Solution of the Jewish question were established through the isolation of the Jewish population in ghettos, surrounded by walls, and through the Declaration of Identification, which forced all Jews to display a yellow Star of David. The Jewish ghettos in the Generalgouvernement area of Poland (the area of German-occupied Poland – see Map 2 – which was not integrated into the Reich and which became a dumping ground for unwanted Poles and Jews) became giant concentration camps, overseen by Jewish councils (*Judenrate*), whose actions were controlled by Nazi officials. The conditions within the ghettos, which were effectively quarantined small suburbs, were quite appalling.

The establishment of ghettos in Poland was a major downward step towards eventual mass extermination. They were like a waiting room towards the Final Solution of the Jewish question. Many resettled Poles were also placed in large transit camps, which, in terms of the horrendous degradation of life, resembled the ghettos. In the Warsaw ghetto, hundreds of thousands of Jews died from what the Nazis called 'natural causes' – most notably starvation and socially engineered disease.[8] As far as possible, open confrontation by Jews with their

Head of the SS Heinrich Himmler (left) and his deputy, Reinhard Heydrich, in Vienna, 1938. Himmler did more than any other Nazi to carry out the 'Final Solution'. Following the surrender of Germany in 1945, he committed suicide after being captured by the British. Heydrich was assassinated in Prague in 1942 by Czech freedom fighters, an act which provoked savage reprisals, including the destruction of the villages of Lidice and Lezaky.

Nazi tormentors was avoided, but there was considerable opposition in the ghettos, ranging from the maintenance of outlawed religious practices to the creation of escape networks and several armed uprisings. In 1943, some 60,000 Jews in the Warsaw ghetto turned on the Nazis and mounted a bold uprising, which was brutally suppressed by the SS.

The movement towards the Final Solution

Between September 1939 and June 1941 Nazi leaders considered a number of policies to deal with the Jewish question. It was the human chaos within the Generalgouvernement area of Poland, caused by a mass influx of Jews and other resettled ethnic minorities (most notably Poles), which helped force the Nazi regime to move beyond the ghetto system towards mass killing. Before this happened, serious consideration was given to a number of other policy options. One policy, originally favoured by Hitler, was to settle the 'Jewish problem' by rounding up all the Jews of Europe and transporting them to the island of Madagascar, where they would be held under SS control as human hostages to be bargained over in a future peace settlement. The 'Madagascar Plan' was not completely abandoned by Hitler until 10 February 1942. A second policy, which Hitler considered with SS leaders in the spring of 1941, was the physical elimination of the Jews of Europe through mass extermination. Some time between the end of 1940 and June 1941 Hitler came to support the physical extermination of all European Jews, probably under pressure from Himmler and the Nazi authorities in Poland. A third policy also considered – and partly adopted – was to use the Jews as 'slave labour' and literally work them to death. It must be appreciated that the Final Solution of the Jewish question involved both slave labour and extermination running simultaneously.

There appears little doubt that Hitler ordered the mass extermination of Jews, probably in May 1941, but the actual document has never been found. As a result, we do not know whether Hitler gave the go-ahead to plans put forward by Himmler and the SS, or whether he was the sole initiator of the policy. At the Nuremberg trials of Nazi war criminals at the end of the war, those closely involved in the extermination camps spoke of the Final Solution being the implementation of 'a direct order from the Führer'.[9] In June 1941, Himmler, probably acting under the order of Hitler, told the commandant of the Auschwitz concentration camp to construct massive gas chambers for extermination purposes. Yet whether Hitler (not Himmler) was the driving force behind the Final Solution remains a matter of dispute.

The transition to systematic extermination: mass shootings in the Soviet Union

The invasion of the Soviet Union in June 1941 opens up another critical phase of Nazi racial policy: indiscriminate mass killing on a huge scale outside the rules of warfare established at Geneva. This killing was carried out by four specially created SS operational execution units (*Einsatzgruppen A–D*), which had previously operated in Poland to kill 'political opponents' and to round up Jews, but which were now enhanced and deployed to much greater effect in the Soviet Union. The *Einsatzgruppen*, under the control of Heydrich, consisted of members of the *Waffen-SS* (the military wing of the SS), the Gestapo, the Criminal Police (*Sipo*), and the civilian Order Police (*Ordnungspolizei*), composed of officers recruited from the uniformed German police (*Schutzpolizei*) and the rural police (*Gendarmerie*). A large number of technical and administrative personnel were also involved. It was once thought only radical Nazis in the SS and SD were involved in major genocide operations, but it is now clear a very large number of ordinary German personnel were involved.

The *Einsatzgruppen* were mobile killing units which followed behind the German army during the advance across the Soviet Union in 1941. Often with the help of the army, they rounded up Red Army officers, Communist officials and Jews in preparation for execution. Those chosen were marched to the edge of towns and ordered to dig mass graves, strip naked and stand on the edge of these killing pits to be mown down by machine gun fire. Within a mere five months of the start of the German attack on the Soviet Union over 500,000 Jews were killed in similar mass executions.

Ultimately, the *Einsatzgruppen* were responsible for the murder of in excess of 1.2 million Jews in the Soviet Union.[10] Mass mobile shootings on such a scale proved costly and psychologically taxing. The deployment of special gassing vans did not fully meet the need for a more co-ordinated method of mass killing. Even Himmler almost fainted when he witnessed a mass execution of Jews in Minsk in August 1941, and he commented that a more 'humane' method of killing must be found.

The Wannsee conference (1942)

By the end of 1941, the Final Solution of the 'Jewish problem' had come to encompass the mass extermination of all European Jews. Once this decision was taken, more co-ordinated plans were necessary. On 20 January 1942 leading officials involved in the Final Solution met in the Berlin suburb of Wannsee to map out a coherent and efficient programme 'for exterminating the Jews'. Reinhard Heydrich, head of the SD, told the meeting that the ultimate aim of the Final Solution was to exterminate all 11 million Jews in Europe. All Jews in Europe would be brought to Poland. Those fit enough would be worked to death as slave labour and the rest exterminated. The process towards this Final Solution still remains unclear. Before the Wannsee conference there had been a large number of haphazard initiatives and a great deal of improvisation. It was not until the spring of 1942 that a programme of mass extermination was put in place by the Nazi regime which made killing part of the industrial process of war.

The administration of death

Following the Wannsee conference, Nazi mass murder became planned and organised by Adolf Eichmann. Individual concern for the victims was completely repressed or ignored by all those involved. Many Germans shared the awesome burden of responsibility with the Nazi regime for this mass murder. The co-operation of a host of different civilian agencies was also crucial for extermination on the scale envisaged. Trains were booked through travel agencies and each victim was actually charged at 4 pfennigs per kilometre for their one-way ticket to oblivion. Industrial companies built the extermination camps. I. G. Farben licensed the production of the deadly hydrogen-cyanide pellets (trade name Zyclon B) – used for gassing victims – to subsidiary companies. German health experts and doctors worked out how much gas was required to kill a set amount of people. The clothes, hair, false teeth, gold fillings and jewellery of the victims were recycled for profit. The SS were in control of the camps, but the Order Police, recruited in a haphazard manner from the civilian police force, played a central role in transporting the Jewish population to the camps, acting as guards and helping to carry out the killings. In short, thousands of ordinary railway workers and policemen, hundreds of managers, businessmen, administrators and civil servants kept the process of extermination in motion.

In this cold, calculated and detached manner, the government of Nazi Germany made murder part of its everyday policies. In effect, the Nazi state freed those who participated in the killing from any moral responsibility for their actions. In spite of the enormous number of people involved in implementing the Final Solution, and the many millions more who heard the rumours of it, the Nazis still tried to keep the entire operation a secret. Victims were only told they were being 'resettled'. The deception of the victims was carried on to ensure their compliance and thereby aid the efficient running of the extermination process.[11]

The extermination camps

The most horrific aspect of the Nazi death machine were the six purpose-built death camps, at Auschwitz-Birkenau (also a major slave labour camp), Belzec, Chelmno, Majdanek, Sobibor and Treblinka. These six camps have a special importance because they were dedicated, almost exclusively, to the murder of Jews. By the spring of 1942, gas chambers, with adjacent crematoria, were operational in all the camps, except Chelmno, which carried out killings with gas vans.

All the six major extermination centres were located in the Generalgouvernement in Poland, which became a vast dumping ground for all those whose lives the Nazi regime had defined as either 'worthless' or who could be used for slave labour. The most renowned Nazi factory of death was Auschwitz-Birkenau, which had four huge gas chambers with the technical capacity to kill 20,000 people per day. It appears the actual total achieved was nearer 6,000 deaths per day. The scale of the killing operation at Auschwitz-Birkenau can be illustrated by the fact that it was served by 44 parallel railway tracks (twice as many as New York's massive Pennsylvania Station).

Those Jews arriving at Auschwitz-Birkenau came in sealed trains. On the railway platform, they were divided into those fit for slave labour and those – usually children, the sick and the elderly – who were sent immediately to the extermination chambers. Each Jew was tattooed on the arm with a number. A fit, especially a skilled Jewish worker stood a chance of survival (provided he or she remained fit). Out of 35,000 Jewish slave labourers hired by I. G. Farben, at Auschwitz-Birkenau, 10,000 survived.

At Auschwitz-Birkenau, the victims were fooled into thinking they were being taken for a shower. The gas chambers were innocent-looking buildings from the outside, surrounded by well-kept lawns and flower beds. The signs over the entry to the gas chambers read: SHOWERS. Inside, light music was played by a small orchestra of young women dressed in white blouses and navy blue skirts. Victims were told they should undress to get ready for a shower. As they entered the large 'shower room', in company with 2,000 others, large doors clanged shut

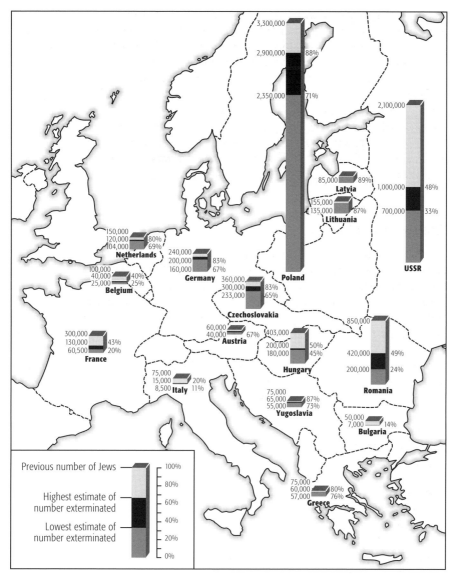

Map 3. Estimates of the numbers of Jews killed in the Holocaust. Source: T. Kirk, *The Longman companion to Nazi Germany.*

behind them. The deadly Zyclon B pellets were dropped through vents above and entered the shower room as deadly cyanide gas. As the gas engulfed the room, panic and screaming broke out. It sometimes took 20 to 30 minutes for the screaming to stop. At this point, every innocent victim was dead. When the door was opened, human bodies were piled high on top of each other, after the desperate attempt of victims to escape from the gas. The task of piling the victims into small wagons and taking them to the adjacent crematoria was

These inmates of Buchenwald Camp, liberated by American troops on 11 April 1945, survived, in Winston Churchill's words, 'the methodical, merciless butchery' of the Nazi killing machine.

carried out by strong Jewish camp inmates, who were promised survival in return for carrying out this grim task. The total number of Jews killed at Auschwitz-Birkenau between 1942 and 1944 (when the camp ceased its killing operations) was 2.5 million executed by gassing, with a further 500,000 dying of shooting and starvation. Map 3 shows estimates of the total number of Jews killed in the Holocaust.

The broader dimensions of Nazi genocide

The death camps which killed Jews have been the major focus of attention. But we should remember that approximately 7 million non-Jews, mostly Russians, Poles and Slavs, were also killed both in systematic and in haphazard ways by the Nazi regime during the Second World War. The total number of dead will never be fully known.[12] There were over 5,800 different Nazi camps in Poland alone, including forced labour camps, ghetto camps, deportation camps, resettlement camps, prisoner of war camps, concentration camps and death camps. In all these camps there was starvation, arbitrary killing and mass extermination using a variety of methods.

Under the conditions of war Nazi Germany reintroduced slave labour on a truly monumental scale in central and eastern Europe. The death-rate of slave labourers, drawn from eastern Europe, was quite staggering. The entire Nazi camp system was a world in which there were no laws, no rules, no restraint, little food, brutal punishment, medical experiments and arbitrary killing. The Germans were the masters and the inmates were the slaves. In all camps, there were different methods of killing: mass shootings, burning, beating to death, hanging, stabbing and medical experiments. There were 4 million Soviet prisoners of war, 2.2 million non-Jewish Poles, 400,000 Gypsies, 2,000 Jehovah's Witnesses, thousands of homosexuals and Freemasons, over 200,000 handicapped people and untold numbers of mentally ill people killed by the Nazi regime. Nazi racial policy classed Jews, Slavs, Gypsies, homosexuals, Bolsheviks and the physically and mentally handicapped as having 'lives unworthy to be lived'.

We can only wonder which group the Nazis would have singled out next for mass extermination if Germany had won the war. Hans Frank, Nazi governor in the Generalgouvernement area of occupied Poland, said: 'Once we have won the war, then, for all I care, mincemeat can be made of Poles, Ukrainians and all the others who run around here.'[13] The treatment of Soviet prisoners of war in Nazi hands was quite appalling. Between 1941 and 1942, 2.8 million Soviet prisoners of war were allowed to starve to death, in truly horrific conditions, in prisoner of war compounds. Many were subjected to torture, beatings, hanging, gassing and medical experiments. The camp, slave labour and ghetto systems of Nazi rule were part of a genocide process which selected many 'racial' groups as ripe for extermination and saw the human life of the people of eastern Europe as expendable.

The singular fate of the Jews

Yet the largest group to suffer from Nazi mass murder were the estimated 6 million Jews who perished. In 1939, there were 9 million Jews living in Europe, but in 1945 there were less than 3 million left alive. In the eyes of Hitler, the Jews were a people who ought not to exist in the world, and the Nazi regime created a vast system of death to try to ensure they did not exist. The Jews were treated much worse than any other group in all the Nazi camps – and, given the absolutely appalling manner in which most other Nazi victims were treated, that says a lot. The Final Solution of the 'Jewish question' was pursued, often against economic logic, when Germany headed for military defeat. It seems Nazi racial dogma viewed the extermination of the Jews as a racial victory, pursued in the midst of a military defeat. Himmler told a group of SS leaders in 1943 that the mass extermination of the Jews was a 'glorious page in your history, which never has been written and never can be'.[14] Himmler later implored SS leaders to carry the secret of the Holocaust 'to our graves'.[15] On 2 November 1944, Himmler suddenly ordered the gassing to stop. On 26 November 1944, he ordered all of the gas chambers to be dismantled and all remaining evidence destroyed. This decision was taken because the Nazi regime was losing the war and knew they faced being put on trial for their dreadful crimes.

The mass killing undertaken by the Nazi regime shows how easily people can delude themselves into thinking modern technology is always beneficial. Modern technology was used by the Nazi regime systematically to kill millions of defenceless people. If the Nazi regime had not been defeated in the Second World War, then many millions more people would have been singled out in further bouts of 'ethnic cleansing'. Where it would have all ended . . . no one really knows.

Document case study
The road to Auschwitz

7.1 Anti-Semitism in Germany: a German woman remembers

I had heard from the example of my parents [who were Nazi supporters] that one could have anti-Semitic opinions without this interfering in one's personal relations with individual Jews. There may appear to be a vestige of tolerance in this attitude, but it is really just this confusion which I blame for the fact that I later contrived to dedicate body and soul to an inhuman political system, without this giving me doubts about my individual decency. In preaching that all the misery of nations was due to the Jews or that the Jewish spirit was seditious and Jewish blood was corrupting, I was not compelled to think of old Herr Lewy or Rosel Cohn [two Jewish people who lived nearby]: I thought only of the bogey-man, 'The Jew'. And when I learned that Jews were being driven from their professions and homes and imprisoned in ghettos, the points switched automatically in my mind to steer round the thought that such a fate could also have overtaken . . . old Lewy. It was only 'the Jew' who was being persecuted and made harmless.

Source: Melita Maschmann, *Account rendered*, London, 1964, pp. 56–57

7.2 A secret Social Democratic Party report on the reaction of ordinary Germans to the Nuremberg Laws, September 1935

The Jewish laws are not taken very seriously because the population has other problems on its mind and is mostly of the opinion that the whole fuss about the Jews is only being made to divert attention from other things and to provide the SA with something to do. But one must not imagine that the anti-Jewish agitation does not have the desired effect on many people. On the contrary, there are enough people who are influenced by the defamation of the Jews and regard the Jews as the originators of many bad things. They have become fanatical opponents of the Jews. This enmity often finds expression in the form of spying on people and denouncing them in public.

Source: J. Noakes and G. Pridham (eds.), *Nazism 1919–1945. A documentary reader, Vol. 2: State, economy and society*, Exeter, 1984, p. 545

7.3 *Kristallnacht*: the evidence of the American consul in Leipzig, November 1938

The shattering of shop windows, looting of stores and dwellings which began in the early hours of 10 November 1938, was hailed subsequently in the Nazi press as a 'spontaneous wave of righteous indignation throughout Germany, as a result of the cowardly Jewish murder of Third Secretary von Rath in the German Embassy in Paris'. So far as a very high percentage of the German people is concerned, a state of popular indignation that would spontaneously lead to such excesses, can be considered as non-existent. On the contrary, in viewing the ruins and attendant measures employed, all of the local crowds observed were obviously benumbed over what had happened and aghast over the unprecedented fury of Nazi acts that had been or were taking place with bewildering rapidity throughout the city.

Source: J. Noakes and G. Pridham (eds.), *Nazism 1919–1945. A documentary reader, Vol. 2: State, economy and society*, Exeter, 1984, pp. 554–55

7.4 Heydrich's orders to the *Einsatzgruppen* in the Soviet Union, June 1941

The following will be executed:
All officials of the Comintern (most of these will be career politicians); Officials of senior and middle rank and 'extremists' in the party, the Central Committee, and the provincial and district committees; the People's Commissars: Jews in the service of the Party or the State; Other extremist elements (saboteurs, propagandists, snipers, assassins, agitators, etc.), in so far as in individual cases they are not required, or are no longer required, for political intelligence of special importance, for future security police measures, or for the economic rehabilitation of the occupied territories . . . No steps will be taken to interfere with any purges that may be initiated by anti communist elements in the newly occupied territories. On the contrary, these are to be secretly encouraged.

Source: H. Buchheim, M. Broszat, H. Krausnick and H-A. Jacobsen, *Anatomy of the SS state*, London, 1968, pp. 62–63

7.5 The murder of Jews by the *Einsatzgruppen*: a contemporary report from *Ensatzgruppe C*, Ukraine, November 1941

As far as the actual executive actions are concerned, the Commandos of the Einsatzgruppe have liquidated around 80,000 persons up to now . . . The largest of these actions took place immediately after the capture of Kiev . . . The difficulties . . . as regards getting hold of them [Jews] were overcome in Kiev by putting up wall posters inviting the Jews to be resettled. Although initially we only expected about 5–6,000 Jews would report, 30,000 Jews turned up who, as a result of a clever piece of organisation, still believed they were going to be resettled until just before their execution. Although up to now 75,000 Jews have been liquidated in this fashion, it must surely be clear that it does not provide a feasible solution of the Jewish Question. It is true that we have succeeded in achieving a total solution of the Jewish question, above all in the smaller towns and in the villages. However, in larger towns we continually find that, although all the Jews have disappeared after such an execution, if a commando returns after a certain interval, he keeps finding Jews in numbers which considerably exceed those who have been executed.

Source: J. Noakes and G. Pridham (eds.), *Nazism 1919–1945. A documentary reader, Vol. 3: Foreign policy, war and racial extermination*, Exeter, 1988, p. 1095

7.6 Hitler's order for the Final Solution: the evidence of Rudolf Höss, camp commandant of Auschwitz, Nuremberg trial, 1946

In the summer of 1941, I cannot remember the exact date, I was suddenly summoned to the Reichsführer SS, directly by his adjunct's office. Contrary to his usual caution, Himmler received me without his adjutant being present and said to me in effect: 'The Führer has ordered that the Jewish question be solved once and for all and we, the SS, are to implement that order. The existing extermination centres in the east are not in a position to carry out the large actions which are anticipated. I have therefore earmarked Auschwitz for this purpose.'

Source: J. Noakes and G. Pridham (eds.), *Nazism 1919–1945. A documentary reader, Vol. 3: Foreign policy, war and racial extermination*, Exeter, 1988, pp. 1105–06.

7.7 A Jewish survivor describes arriving at the extermination camp in Treblinka

When the train arrived in Treblinka I can remember seeing great piles of clothing. Now we feared that the rumours really had been true. I remember saying to my wife more or less: this is the end . . . I can remember the terrible confusion when the doors were pulled open in Treblinka. The Germans and Ukrainians shouted 'get out, out' . . . Then the people who had arrived began to scream and complain. I can remember that whips were used on us. Then, we were told: 'Men to the right, women to the left and get undressed'. My little daughter who was with me then ran to her mother when we were separated. I never saw them again and could not even say good bye. Then, while I was undressing I was selected by a German to be a so called work-Jew.

Source: J. Noakes and G. Pridham (eds.), *Nazism 1919–1945. A documentary reader, Vol. 3: Foreign policy, war and racial extermination*, Exeter, 1988, pp. 1154–55

7.8 The killing process: the evidence of a Jewish doctor at Auschwitz-Birkenau

The men stood on one side, the women on the other. They were addressed in a very polite and friendly way: 'You have been on a journey. You are dirty. You will take a bath. Get undressed quickly.' Towels and soap were handed out, and then suddenly the brutes woke up and showed their true faces; this horde of people, these men and women were driven outside with hard blows and forced both summer and winter to go the few hundred metres to the 'Shower Room'. Above the entry door was the word 'Shower'. One could see shower heads on the ceiling which were cemented in but never had water flowing through them. These poor innocents were crammed together, pressed against each other. Then panic broke out, for at last they realised the fate in store for them. But blows with rifle butts and revolver shots soon restored order and finally they all entered the death chamber. The doors were then shut and, ten minutes later, the temperature was high enough to facilitate the condensation of the hydrogen cyanide, for the condemned were gassed with hydrogen cyanide . . . [thrown] in through a little vent . . . This was the so called 'Zyclon B', gravel pellets saturated with twenty per cent of hydrogen cyanide which was used by the German barbarians . . . One could hear fearful screams, but a few moments later there was complete silence. Twenty to twenty five minutes later, the doors and windows were opened to ventilate the rooms and the corpses were thrown at once into pits to be burned.

Source: J. Noakes and G. Pridham (eds.), *Nazism 1919–1945. A documentary reader, Vol. 3: Foreign policy, war and racial extermination*, Exeter, 1988, p. 1180

Document case-study questions

1 What does 7.1 tell us about the reaction of ordinary Germans towards the growth of anti-Semitism in Nazi Germany?

2 Comment on what 7.2 tells us about public opinion in Germany towards Nazi anti-Jewish legislation.

3 What insights does 7.3 provide into the reaction of ordinary Germans towards *Kristallnacht*?

4 In light of 7.4, would you suggest Nazi execution squads in the Soviet Union made Jews the chief priority of their operations?

5 Explain the main differences between the orders of the *Einsatzgruppen* as outlined in 7.4 and how they were carried out by *Einsatzgruppe C* as outlined in 7.5.

6 What reservations do you have about 7.6 as evidence that Hitler did give the decisive order for the implementation of the Final Solution?

7 How does 7.7 convey the impending horror of the victims of the Holocaust?

8 What impressions do you get of the plight of the victims of Nazi mass murder from 7.8?

Notes and references

1 Jewish writers also use the term *Shoah*, signifying catastrophic destruction, to describe Nazi mass murder of the Jews.

2 M. Burleigh and W. Wippermann, *The racial state: Germany 1933–1939*, Cambridge, 1991, p. 39.

3 See D. J. Goldhagen, *Hitler's willing executioners. Ordinary Germans and the Holocaust*, London, 1996, pp. 49–79.

4 *Ibid.*

5 See K. Schleunes, *The twisted road to Auschwitz. Nazi policy towards the Jews*, London, 1965.

6 For a detailed discussion see P. Burrin, *Hitler and the Jews. The genesis of the Holocaust*, London, 1993.

7 See M. Burleigh, *Death and deliverance 'euthanasia' in Germany 1900–1945*, Cambridge, 1994.

8 R. Hilberg, *The destruction of the European Jews*, Vol. 3, New York, 1985, pp. 480–85.

9 J. Noakes and G. Pridham (eds.), *Nazism 1919–1945. A documentary reader*, Vol. 3: *Foreign policy, war and racial extermination*, Exeter, 1988, pp. 1105–06.

10 Z. Gitelman, 'The Soviet politics of the Holocaust', in J. E. Young (ed.), *The art of memory. Holocaust memorials in history*, New York, 1994, p. 140.

11 See H. Arendt, *Eichmann in Jerusalem: a report on the banality of evil*, London, 1977.

12 It is now agreed that 13 million is a reasonable estimate. See D. Weinberg and B. L. Sherwin, 'The Holocaust: historical overview', in B. L. Sherwin and S. G. Ament (eds.), *Encountering the Holocaust: an interdisciplinary survey*, London, 1979, p. 22.

13 Quoted in J. A. Lukacs, *The great powers and eastern Europe*, New York, 1970, p. 570.

14 K. Hildebrand, *The Third Reich*, London, 1984, p. 72.

15 *Ibid.*

8 The verdict of historians

The problems of debate

The historical debate over Nazi Germany is like no other, not merely because of the high level of emotion and controversy it has generated, but also for its sheer size. There have been more biographies of Hitler than of any other major historical figure (more than 1,000 at the last count). Among them are hundreds of 'psycho-histories', focusing on the 'mind of Hitler', which seek to explain the horrors of the Nazi regime by reference to Hitler being mad, a psychopath, or a schizophrenic (sometimes all three). It is quite amazing, if we accept these studies, how Hitler avoided being locked up in a mental hospital well before he ever got out of short pants. In addition, over 100,000 studies of various aspects of Nazi Germany have been published.

Historians were writing about Nazi Germany almost as soon as Hitler's death was reported. The immediate question for them was to evaluate whether the Nazi period represented a continuity with, or a unique break from, the course of German history. If Nazism was a unique phenomenon, separated from the rest of German history, it can be treated as an evil desert island, not linked to the German past. In the immediate post-war era historians tended to treat Nazi Germany as a singularly unique phenomenon.

In the 1980s, a group of German historians called for the Nazi period to be examined in the same 'objective' manner as any other period of history. According to Martin Broszat, the evil of the Nazi past has been replayed so often it has lost much of its original unique ability to shock. Broszat claimed it was time for the Nazi period to be analysed like any other period of history, so that long-term trends in German political, social and economic development could be pinpointed.[1] Much more controversy surrounded the view of Ernst Nolte, who claimed that the original idea for a Final Solution did not originate with the Nazi regime but was a reaction against the Marxist yearning for the total eradication of the bourgeois class. According to this view, the Holocaust was a pre-emptive defensive strike by Hitler against what he saw as the ultimate aim of 'Judaeo-Bolshevism': to destroy the bourgeois class in every country in the world.[2]

Not surprisingly, these attempts to 'normalise' the Nazi era have been fiercely resisted. Saul Friedländer suggested that attempts by German historians to normalise the Nazi era could lead to Hitler's 'war against the Jews' being seen as not much different in essence from other examples of genocide or ethnic cleansing committed by other 'evil' regimes during the twentieth century.[3] The heated 'historians' debate' (the *Historikerstreit*) revealed once again how difficult it is to apply the normal historical tools of rational analysis, objectivity and moral detachment to the study of Nazi Germany.[4]

What is most surprising about the study of Nazi Germany is the extremely fragmentary nature of the source materials relating to Adolf Hitler's role as dictator. A great deal of crucial information was deliberately destroyed by the Nazi regime or else was lost in bombing raids. It is very difficult to know exactly how decisions were arrived at by Hitler or carried out according to his wishes. The inadequacy of the available source materials helps to explain why there has been so much controversy in almost every area of debate over Nazi Germany. The aim of this concluding chapter is to evaluate some of the key historical debates surrounding the history of Nazi Germany.

Adolf Hitler: master of Nazi Germany?

The most dominating figure in all the historical studies of Nazi Germany is Adolf Hitler. Any study which puts Hitler's aims and personality at the centre of analysis is usually described as 'Hitlocentric' or 'intentionalist'. A typical example of this approach was put forward by Hugh Trevor Roper (Lord Dacre), who portrayed Hitler as 'the complete master' of Nazi Germany, following a consistent programme of ideas outlined in *Mein Kampf*.[5] A variation of this 'intentionalist' interpretation was advanced by Alan Bullock, who also viewed Hitler as the dominant figure in Nazi Germany, but who saw the Nazi dictator as flexible in pursuit of his ultimate goals, which were primarily in the field of foreign affairs and territorial conquest. According to this view, Hitler's so-called 'revolution' was 'wanton destruction' in pursuit of greater and greater power.[6]

In more recent times, there has developed a 'structuralist/functionalist' approach to the study of Nazi Germany, which attempts to locate Hitler within the complex power structure of the Nazi state. The structuralists/functionalists emphasise the bohemian nature of Hitler's lifestyle and show his lack of involvement in the day-to-day running of the Nazi state. Broszat depicts Hitler as a 'weak dictator', who was never in complete control of the government machine in Nazi Germany. Hitler had very little idea about how to create an efficient and distinctive Nazi system of government. In Broszat's view, Hitler was really a greedy power seeker who operated as a referee in bitter disputes between competing agencies of government.[7] Ian Kershaw has recently shown a clear distinction between the powerful propaganda 'myth' of Adolf Hitler as the all-powerful dictator and the 'reality' of the Nazi government system, which was a chaotic maze of overlapping, conflicting and often contradictory spheres of authority.[8]

The structuralist/functionalist approach has the advantage of showing the complex nature of Nazi decision making. It also reveals how individuals and agencies were allowed a wide degree of flexibility in carrying out 'the Führer's will'. Yet the idea of Hitler as a 'weak dictator' has not been accepted. Karl Dietrich Bracher has recently emphasised that the chaotic nature of Nazi government – which structuralists/functionalists have concentrated upon – was actually a deliberate ploy by Hitler to 'divide and rule' by playing one ineffective minister off against another, and pitting one power group against another, while ensuring he remained in a completely dominant position within the state. According to this view, Hitler's rule was a deliberately planned form of controlled chaos.[9]

Foreign policy

The role Hitler played in the German road to war is another feature of the historical debate. This debate has long been dominated by the view that the major cause of the Second World War was Hitler's burning desire for territorial expansion. The main disagreement among historians concerns the importance of Hitler's aims for German foreign policy. The orthodox position on Hitler's foreign policy aims was originally advanced by Hugh Trevor Roper, who suggested Hitler followed a consistent, unchanging, programme of territorial expansion laid out in *Mein Kampf*. The three most important aims of Hitler's foreign policy were to overturn the Treaty of Versailles, gain *Lebensraum* in eastern Europe through a conquest of the Soviet Union and to search for the Final Solution to the 'Jewish question'.[10]

This orthodox 'intentionalist' interpretation has been challenged, but not fundamentally altered. It seems there were intelligible goals in Hitler's foreign policy. He did wish to acquire *Lebensraum* in eastern Europe at the expense of the Soviet Union and was willing to risk a general war to achieve this objective. Jäckel views Hitler's ideas as a guideline for his foreign policy actions, which were often adapted to deal with specific problems.[11] The idea of a gradual, stage-by-stage foreign policy plan (*Stufenplan*), originally put forward by Hillgruber, has come to be widely accepted by foreign policy specialists. Hillgruber argues that Hitler followed a three-stage plan which aimed first to engage in a war of territorial conquest to gain German dominance in Europe, followed by a second conflict to gain territory in the Middle East and finally a war for global domination against the USA.[12] The only question to be resolved is whether Hitler wanted European domination or world domination. Most supporters of the 'intentionalist' view depict Hitler's foreign policy as the outcome of his own personal aims, which were implemented with a high degree of tactical opportunism and flexibility.

At the other side of the debate on Hitler's foreign policy are 'revisionist' (often termed structuralist/functionalist) historians, who reject the idea of Hitler following a unique and deeply personal set of foreign policy aims which were pursued consistently and systematically. Bracher suggested Hitler's foreign policy had no overall design, was subject to internal pressure and was mostly a diversion from the chaos within Nazi Germany.[13] Hans-Adolf Jacobsen has shown the structure of foreign policy under Hitler resembled 'administrative chaos', often being influenced by a number of separate and often competing agencies.[14] Broszat accepts the Nazi regime was geared towards war, but he does not believe there was a detailed 'master plan' behind Hitler's foreign policy, only a burning desire to maintain a forward momentum for the Nazi regime through foreign policy success.[15] Hans Mommsen describes Hitler's foreign policy as an ill-thought-out, very poorly planned 'expansion without object', a sort of escape hatch from the confused domestic policy of the Nazi regime. According to this view, Hitler kept on moving compulsively forward, with little idea of where he was going, nor with any idea of when he was eventually going to stop.[16]

The most controversial 'revisionist' view of Hitler's foreign policy was advanced by A. J. P. Taylor,[17] who claimed that Hitler was no ice-cold planner, but acted on the spur of the moment in following a foreign policy not very different from that of earlier German governments. Taylor suggested the Second World War broke out by accident in September 1939, not because Hitler planned it, or even wanted it, but because of the blunders caused by British and French attempts to find a way of stopping him. Taylor describes Hitler's foreign policy ideas as 'day dreams'. In his view, Hitler's foreign policy succeeded for a while because of his ability to seize opportunities and to profit from the diplomatic errors and mistakes of his opponents.

The 'revisionist' interpretation of Hitler's foreign policy has been severely criticised on three counts:

1 for overlooking the high degree of autonomy and control which Hitler exercised over foreign policy;
2 for consistently failing to prove that Hitler did not exercise what amounted to 'personal rule' in foreign policy;
3 for failing to reveal how domestic or economic factors limited Hitler's control over foreign policy actions or decisions.

Another key aspect of this historical debate concerns the issue of whether Hitler's foreign policy had similar aims to those of previous German governments. The idea of 'continuity' was most forcefully expressed by Fritz Fischer, who claimed that German foreign policy from 1871 to 1945 changed in form, but not in aims.[18] This view was supported by Hans-Ulrich Wehler, who viewed German foreign policy from Bismarck to Hitler as primarily a diversion from internal tension and designed to preserve the power exercised by the ruling army/land-owning/industrial elites. According to this view, Hitler's foreign policy was an extreme version of the long-held German desire to create an empire in eastern Europe.[19]

It seems that many of Hitler's so-called unique foreign policy aims were very similar to what had gone before. Domination of eastern Europe was a key aim of the German government during the First World War. The very areas which Hitler designated to come under German control at the end of a successful war against the Soviet Union were exactly the same areas taken under German control by the terms of the Treaty of Brest-Litovsk (1918). The concept of *Lebensraum*, central to Hitler's foreign policy aims, has been traced back to the writings of the Pan-German League before 1914.

Nonetheless, many historians have disputed the idea of a continuity in German foreign policy under Hitler. Geoffrey Eley, though willing to accept there were some elements of continuity, emphasised that Hitler's foreign policy aims were 'more extreme in every way' than those supported by traditional German elites before 1933. Eley suggests that Hitler combined expansion with extermination in a manner never contemplated by previous German leaders.[20] It seems the members of the old German elites in the army and industry were always fearful about Hitler's eventual destination and the methods he used to get there. Hillgruber argues that the three ultimate objectives of Hitler's foreign policy – world domination, a world purged of Jews and the creation of biological elite – amount to a unique and revolutionary foreign policy, alien to German tradition.[21]

A social revolution?

Another key area of historical debate concerns the impact of Nazi rule on German society. Some historians believe Nazism produced 'revolutionary' changes in German society, while others have suggested it was a 'counter-revolutionary', negative and destructive movement which changed very little. Changes in social attitudes and values are notoriously difficult to calculate. We must also remember that the Nazi regime lasted a mere 12 years. The very term 'revolution' is increasingly losing explanatory value for historians because it seems to imply a complete transformation of society. Even the term 'counter-revolution' is fraught with difficulty, as it implies a turning back of the clock to practices of a previous era.

The most well-known supporter of the view that Hitler's regime produced a social revolution in German society is the political scientist Ralf Dahrendorf, who claimed at the heart of the 'German problem' lay the dominance of the traditional German elites, who were all opposed to modern industrial development and democracy. Dahrendorf claimed the Nazi regime did progressively break the stranglehold of these 'semi-feudal' elites between 1933 and 1945, thereby unwittingly paving the way towards the economic modernisation of German industry and society in the post-war era.[22]

This argument found support from David Schoenbaum, who confined his analysis of social change in Nazi Germany to the period 1933 to 1939. Schoenbaum suggested that the Nazi regime destroyed the traditionally hierarchical nature of German society, putting in its place a more classless idea of society, which encouraged greater industrial modernisation and improved social mobility. According to this view, Nazism was really a failed attempt to halt the march of modern industrial society, which in the process of its dynamic march forward produced a 'revolution of destruction' which left Germany as a modern industrial and urban society.[23]

One of the central problems with both these interpretations is the way they suggest the Nazi social 'revolution' was a revolution by default. They suggest it was an unwanted by-product of the contradictory aims of Nazi ideology, which wanted to create a friendly folk community of patriotic and classless Germans living on the soil, but proposed to reach this Nazi utopia by gaining living space with modern weapons, produced by modern industry.

A great many historians remain sceptical about the idea of a social revolution in Nazi Germany. They have suggested that Nazi social policy was window dressing for the real objective, which was to strengthen the position of capitalist monopolies and to uphold class differences. Some Marxist historians went further, by claiming that the Nazi regime – in spite of its popular appeal to some sections of German society – was the political strong arm of a counter-revolution which favoured German monopoly capitalists and the military – a sort of military–capitalist junta. It was a regime which brutally deprived the working class of all political representation and all existing trade union and employment rights.

Marxist views on Nazi Germany are usually depicted as 'simplistic' and 'vulgar' by traditional 'liberal-bourgeois' historians, and have not been accepted in the mainstream of the debate. Yet the idea of left-wing historians that Hitler's regime was a power coalition involving big business and the army is becoming increasingly more attractive. It seems that Hitler was by no means a radical Nazi on economic or social policy, but a rather moderate, even a conservative one. A true Nazi 'social revolution' – the one Nazi radicals such as Röhm, Strasser and many other grass-roots members wanted – would have turned the army into a people's army, run by the Nazi SA, and have placed industry and retailing under state control, and even have redistributed land to the rural peasantry. Yet those Nazis who wanted a Nazi social revolution were the very same people who Hitler had killed during the 'Night of the Long Knives'. Hitler appears to have favoured a power coalition between the Nazi elite, the army and big business rather than creating an outright Nazi society from 1933 to 1939. This view is reinforced by the fact that Hitler proved very reluctant to interfere with the existing social and economic order at the top of German society. The social position of traditional elites remained untouched until the very darkest days of the war. The civil service, the army, the Foreign Office, the judiciary and big business recruited from the same upper-middle-class groups as they had always done. Even the SS – usually viewed as a Nazi organisation – contained among its most elite sections a disproportionate number of members from the old land-owning aristocracy and prominent upper-middle-class families. Even Hitler accepted, towards the end of the war, that he had completely failed to Nazify the high command of the army.

To historians who have examined life inside Nazi Germany, the idea of a Nazi social revolution is even less convincing. Detlev Peukert, in a path-breaking study of everyday life inside Nazi Germany, showed that the German people became more consumer oriented after 1933 than ever before. It seems Nazi Germany produced very little divergence from the earlier development of the country into a modern industrial society, nor did it change the differences, the opportunities and the wealth and property of different class groups. According to Peukert, Hitler's regime actively promoted a consumer-oriented society, with increased welfare benefits for the family and greater leisure opportunities.[24] Winkler claims that the so-called Nazi 'social revolution' was a propaganda myth of the regime which cannot be sustained by a detailed examination of social and economic developments in Germany from 1933 to 1945.[25] Ian Kershaw argues that Nazism 'did not produce a social revolution' but actually 'bolstered the existing class order'. The Nazi era is coming to be viewed as a capitalist–Nazi coalition (supported by the army) against the interests of organised labour; this coalition, according to Kershaw, developed the most 'ruthless and exploitative' type of capitalist rule ever encountered.[26]

The historians and the Nazi economy

Most historians agree that the Nazi regime failed to develop any unique or distinctive economic policies. Hitler saw the successful business person as a 'gifted individual' who had grown rich through talent and hard work. He had no wish to weaken the economic position of such people. The Nazi economy contained elements of capitalist free enterprise, combined with government regulation and expenditure on rearmament and public works. It was a 'third way' between free market capitalism and socialism. According to J. Heyl, Adolf Hitler was an 'economic simpleton' who thought all the problems of Germany could be solved by wars of plunder.[27] The only economic policy Hitler showed any enthusiasm for – the Four Year Plan of 1936 (the drive for economic self-sufficiency) – was a complete failure.

The debate over the role of economic factors in Nazi Germany has been dominated by the relationship between big business and the Nazi regime. Marxist historians have long argued that German monopoly capitalists saw Nazism as a lifeboat to shield them from the stormy waters of free market economic competition and the power of organised labour. According to this view, Hitler was the puppet of German monopoly capitalists. Yet studies of the role of big business and the rise of Hitler have shown the Nazi Party was the last not the first resort for German big business.

Nevertheless, the Nazi regime did provide an economic climate which greatly benefited the financial position of big business. Historians have long debated who was in overall control: Hitler or big business. Hildebrand claims that the Nazi economy was in the service of the foreign policy aims of the regime, while Nolte reckoned that Hitler virtually eliminated industrialists as a major influence within the decision-making process.[28] This widely accepted 'primacy of politics' interpretation of the power structure within Nazi Germany views the decisions of Hitler as independent from, and not determined by, the needs of big business. Richard Overy claims that industry was subordinate to the authority and the interests of the Nazi movement.[29]

Yet William Carr has suggested the attempt to isolate who took the major decisions on economic matters will always produce the same answer – Hitler and the Nazis – but fail to discern the subtle and mutually supportive alliance which existed between big business and the Nazi regime.[30] A. Schweitzer defined the relationship between big business and the Nazi elite as a 'mutually beneficial coalition'.[31] This view is reinforced by the knowledge that many Nazi economic policies greatly favoured big business. The destruction of independent trade unions and the definition of the 'employer' as virtual master of the factory gave capital enormous power over organised labour. The destruction of many resourceful Jewish business competitors also worked to the advantage of large monopoly companies. Robert Brady goes further by portraying Hitler's regime as 'a dictatorship of big business', which organised the economy for the benefit of giant industrial monopolies and hoped to secure new territory to aid the economic expansion of German big business.[32] In wartime, the Nazis even introduced slave labour, which created even greater opportunities for major German companies to exploit workers and make increased profits. A self-sufficient German economic monopoly, using slave labour, would have been the outcome of victory for the Nazis during the Second World War. More recently, a triangular, mutually supportive relationship – 'a bourgeois hegemony'– between big business, the army and the Nazis has been used to describe the power structure of the Nazi economy. Within this relationship, Hitler had great autonomy over the decision-making process, the army grew in strength and big business gained economically from the way Hitler exercised his monopoly of power because he ensured the dominance of capital over labour in the production of goods.

The fundamental differences of approach between Marxist historians, who are heavily theoretical, and liberal historians, who are heavily influenced by the documents, are diametrically at odds, with the result that each side dismisses the conclusions of the other, usually in contemptuous terms. Marxists accuse liberal historians of having their heads buried in the sands of self-justifying documents and of being obsessed with who took decisions, not with the economic beneficiaries of those decisions; liberal historians accuse Marxists of putting forward theories which cannot be supported by evidence.

In more recent examinations of the relationship between big business and the Nazi regime, however, it is coming to be accepted (save for the dinosaurs on each side) that the concepts of a 'primacy of politics' and a 'primacy of economics' are both extremely unsatisfactory tools for explaining the nature of the Nazi economy. A third approach is to accept there was a greater interweaving of aims between major German industrial companies and the Nazi leadership than was previously acknowledged. The crude separation of the political decision makers from the business world is no longer acceptable. According to Volkmann, there was a greater unity of interest between the Nazi state and major industry than has been previously acknowledged.[33] In Kershaw's view, the fact that major monopoly companies were 'the greatest single winners' from the Nazi regime was no accident, but an outcome of the policies followed by the Nazi state.

A second key area of historical debate on the Nazi economy revolves around the issue of whether Hitler's decision for war in 1939 was due to a severe economic crisis in Germany. Tim Mason argued that the headlong drive towards armaments expenditure by the Nazi regime caused severe economic difficulties, only resolvable either by cutting arms expenditure, which Hitler refused to contemplate, or by embarking on limited wars, designed to acquire essential supplies of raw materials to head off impending economic collapse. According to this view, Hitler was compelled by impending economic difficulties to follow the path towards war.[34] In support of this view, David Kaiser has shown how each Nazi occupation helped to secure additional economic resources which did ease economic pressure. Hildebrand has suggested that in 1939 Hitler faced a desperate choice between bankruptcy or war.[35]

On the other hand, Richard Overy has quite convincingly shown that the problems of the German economy in the late 1930s have been exaggerated. It seems they were not so great in 1939 as to require a war of plunder to resolve them.[36] Milward argued that because Germany had gained 'informal' economic dominance over eastern Europe, there was no desperate need to seize Poland in September 1939.[37] These arguments have come to be widely accepted. If Germany wanted a war for pure economic gain in 1939, then Romania, with its vast reserves of oil, or Sweden, a key supplier of iron ore, were much better economic targets. In Overy's view, power-politics predominated over economic considerations in the decision to attack Poland.[38]

A closely related economic sub-debate centres on the type of war Hitler was supposedly preparing for. It has been claimed that the German economy in the late 1930s resembled a war economy in peacetime. It is generally agreed by historians that the type of war the German economy was best suited to was a limited series of short Blitzkrieg-type wars, not a long war. A central feature of this discussion is the significance of the Four Year Plan of 1936. It was claimed by Mason that the introduction of the Four Year Plan pushed the German economy into planned and directed preparations for war. However, Overy has revealed the Four Year Plan was not successful either in gaining complete state control of industry or in preparing the German economy for a long war of attrition. The Four Year Plan reached a mere 6 of the 26 self-sufficiency targets it set out to achieve.[39] It remains doubtful, however, whether economic factors determined Hitler's decision for war in September 1939.

The Holocaust

The most controversial of all the historical debates surrounding Nazi Germany centres on the Holocaust. No aspect of the history of Nazi Germany has been so dominated by non-German historians. No subject has shaken the concept of historical 'objectivity' more fully than discussion of the systematic murder by the Nazi regime. The term 'Holocaust' is used to describe the attempt to execute all Jews in Europe by the Nazis. Some historians prefer to examine the whole programme of death implemented by the regime using the term 'genocide', a less emotive term, which denotes a deliberate programme of killing organised by the state against selected ethnic and political groups.

The historical debate on the Holocaust is dominated by the issue of whether the fate of the Jews under Nazi rule was unique or should be fitted into a broader framework, which includes all those who were singled out for extermination and execution by the regime. There is no doubt that post-war Jewish national identity in Israel is closely linked with the Holocaust, and the desire of Jewish people to

The Allied victors, Great Britain, France, the United States and the Soviet Union, made the unprecedented decision to put leading Nazis on trial for 'war crimes'. A total of 127 German and Austrian political and military leaders were charged. This photograph is of the final session at the Nuremberg War Trials, 1 October 1946. On the front row, left to right: Göring, head of the Luftwaffe (committed suicide in his cell after being sentenced to death); Hess, deputy Führer (life sentence); Ribbentrop, foreign minister (hanged); Keitel, head of chiefs of staff (hanged); Kaltenbrunner, head of security (hanged); Rosenberg, minister for occupied eastern Europe (hanged); Frank, governor of Poland (hanged); Frick, interior minister (hanged); Streicher, publisher of the Nazi organ, *Der Stürmer* (hanged); Funk, economics minister (life sentence); Schacht, economics minister (acquitted).
On the back row: Dönitz, head of German navy and Hitler's successor (life sentence); Raeder, grand admiral (life sentence); Schirach, leader of the Hitler Youth (imprisoned); Sauckel, minister for slave labour (hanged); Jodl, army chief of staff (hanged); von Papen, ex-Chancellor (acquitted); Seyss-Inquart, governor of the Netherlands (hanged); Speer, minister of armaments and munitions (life sentence); von Neurath, *Reichsprotektor* in Bohemia and Moravia until 1941 (imprisoned); Fritzsche, head of radio propaganda (acquitted).

keep the Holocaust as a unique example of Nazi genocide remains powerful. Many historians have questioned this approach and claimed that to argue that the Jews suffered a unique fate under Nazi rule prevents a broader understanding of other victims and comparison with other examples of genocide.

The orthodox interpretation of the Holocaust centres on Hitler's own virulent anti-Semitism and his long-standing desire to find the Final Solution to the

'Jewish question'. This interpretation suggests there was a clear and logical path from Hitler's original anti-Semitic views to planning the physical extermination of Jews during the Second World War. One of the most well-known supporters of this view is Lucy Dawidowicz, who suggests Hitler had a 'grand design' in his head for the destruction of the Jews, possibly dating back to the end of the First World War, which remained a central aim when Hitler came to power. Dawidowicz views the attempt by the Nazi regime to exterminate all Jews in Europe as a unique example of mass murder.[40]

On the other side of the debate are those historians who believe the Holocaust was not unique, nor part of a master plan. Indeed, the idea of the Holocaust developing in accordance with a clear and logical timetable is no longer accepted by a majority of historians. The most influential supporter of this view is Karl Schleunes, who suggests there was a 'twisted road to Auschwitz'.[41] Schleunes suggests that Nazi policy towards the Jews developed in stages. It was accepted by Hitler that the Jews had no place in the long-term future of Germany, but other options – deportation, emigration and forced resettlement – were attempted before he went ahead with the Final Solution. If Hitler had wished all Jews in Europe to be exterminated all along, then why did he let so many flee from Germany before 1939? According to Schleunes, the answer lies in a lack of any real 'grand design' on the part of Hitler for the physical extermination of the Jews before the start of the Second World War.

A great many historians now view the movement towards mass extermination as a cumulative process, greatly influenced by the chaos caused by the vast German expansion in eastern Europe. There is no evidence of a comprehensive Nazi plan to exterminate the Jews before 1941. It is now clear there were different factions within the Nazi regime in competition with each other who wished to implement what they thought was the 'Führer's will' on the 'Jewish question'. Indeed, a great deal of initiative was allowed to local Nazi leaders in the implementation of the Final Solution.

Not surprisingly, Hitler's exact role in the implementation of the Final Solution has been the subject of enormous debate. It is generally accepted that he played a crucial role in rousing anti-Semitism within Germany, thus preparing the ground for the Holocaust. Yet there is very little evidence of Hitler playing a major role in the design or implementation of the actual killing process. It is now clear that the Nazi Party was divided between 'moderates' and 'radicals' over the question of what the Final Solution should be. Schleunes describes Hitler's role in the Holocaust as 'shadowy'. Hitler did often respond to pressure from below within the Nazi movement, especially from the SS–SD–Gestapo–police apparatus and from SA radicals in the localities, to adopt more radical measures on the Jewish question.

Mommsen suggests that the Final Solution 'can by no means by attributed to Hitler alone', even though it is generally accepted that Hitler did order the mass murder, probably in the summer of 1941, and enthusiastically supported it.[42] The most controversial view of Hitler's role in the Holocaust was put forward by David Irving, who suggested that Himmler organised the Final Solution, on his own authority, and did not bother to inform Hitler the killing process was going on until 1943.[43] New evidence from Himmler's diary (recently found in the Soviet archives) has shown Hitler definitely knew in December 1941. A more plausible view of Hitler's role is that of Broszat, who suggested there was no question of downplaying the ultimate responsibility of Hitler for the Final Solution, but he concluded that the policy to exterminate the Jews developed gradually, institutionally, within the Nazi state and was accelerated greatly by the growth in the number of Jews under German rule between 1939 and 1941.[44] It seems that Hitler approved of the Final Solution, but left the major decisions over its implementation to the SS leaders – Himmler and Heydrich.

The question of whether anti-Semitism was the most virulent hatred of Hitler has also been disputed. Arno Mayer has suggested that the major chosen victim for 'extermination' was not the Jews but the Soviet state and its people. In Mayer's view, it was the burning desire of Hitler to gain living space at the expense of the Soviet Union – by completely 'liquidating' the Soviet regime – which began the process of mass Nazi genocide. According to Mayer, without the invasion of the Soviet Union and the lawless actions committed against Russian people, the essential preconditions for the escalation towards a Final Solution would probably not have taken place.[45]

The major problem with Mayer's interpretation is that it ignores Hitler's own conception of 'Marxism' and 'Soviet Bolshevism', which he saw as an integral part of the 'world Jewish conspiracy'. A crucial means of severely weakening the strongest political centre of the 'Jewish world conspiracy', for Hitler, was to crush the Soviet regime. Nevertheless, what Mayer has drawn attention to is whether the Jewish experience under Nazi rule was unique or should be fitted into a broader racial/political programme of genocide. The Russian people became, in Nazi eyes, a conglomeration of three of the most hated 'racial' groups: Bolsheviks, Jews and Slavs. This helps to explain why there was such a lawless disregard for human life by the German army during the invasion of the Soviet Union. The German army used flame throwers to destroy Soviet towns, cities and villages, which had not been used in attacks in western Europe against civilians. The treatment of Soviet prisoners of war, the 'soldiers of Bolshevism', was equally horrendous. The first test of Zyclon B and the first systematic shootings were of Soviet prisoners of war. Indeed, it is estimated that less than 10 per cent of Soviet prisoners of war ever returned home alive – a figure which bears comparison with any type of genocide ever committed by any regime. The Gypsy population of eastern Europe and a large number of Poles suffered a similar fate.

It is also known that Himmler had grand plans to exterminate up to 30 million 'Slavs' throughout Europe in pursuit of the Nazi policy of 'racial hygiene' if Germany had won the war. A whole range of groups – the physically and mentally handicapped, gays and even vagrants – were also marked down for future extermination. It seems that the Nazi defeat in the Second World War helped to prevent a series of new Holocausts. In this way, the Final Solution can be viewed as part of a grandiose plan to create a 'racially pure' Nazi Europe. The aims of Nazi racial policy were probably as boundless as the territorial ambitions of the regime. The use of the terms 'racial policy' and 'genocide' draw attention to the vast scope of the regime's policy of 'racial hygiene' and places the Jewish experience within a broader context, without in any way lessening or diminishing its importance.

The most controversial aspect of the current debate on the Holocaust revolves around the participation of ordinary Germans in the mass killing of Jews. Daniel Goldhagen has recently aroused great controversy by drawing attention to this issue.[46] Goldhagen's study concentrates on the high level of anti-Semitism in Germany, which made the conditions for the elimination of the Jews possible, and on the activities of the *Ordungspolizei*, which was composed not of ideologically committed Nazis but of what he terms 'ordinary Germans'. Goldhagen suggests the role of the Order Police in the Nazi extermination of Jews was as important as that of the SS and the *Einsatzgruppen*. He claims there was a 'straight road' to the Holocaust, which was the inevitable outcome of a long-standing desire shared by Hitler and a great majority of Germans to 'eliminate' Jews from German society. The ordinary Germans who participated in the Holocaust were 'Hitler's willing executioners'.

The whole thrust of Goldhagen's argument is to emphasise that ordinary Germans cannot simply hide behind the idea of the Holocaust as a secret, clandestine activity, carried out by selected members of the criminal Nazi elite. Instead, Germans must face up to a broader 'national' responsibility for what happened. According to Goldhagen, the Holocaust was the inevitable outcome of long-standing anti-Semitic attitudes in German society, and Hitler was merely the catalyst who unleashed these pent-up desires within German society to eliminate the Jews.

This is a very challenging interpretation, which raises the question of collective German guilt for the horrors of the Nazi period. We do know that over 100,000 German people were directly involved in the mass extermination programme. A great many were willing, even enthusiastic, executioners. But to suggest all German people were anti-Semitic not only appears crude but could be seen as a form of anti-German racism. Detlev Peukert has shown that a great many Germans retreated into private worlds during the Nazi era, reluctantly accepting the power but not the ideology of the Nazis. It is highly contentious to suggest either 'anti-Semitism' or the ability to engage in mass killing was a singularly German characteristic. Many non-Germans took part in guarding camps, and many troops from a large number of countries participated in mass executions.

The most vociferous critic of Goldhagen is Christopher Browning, a pioneer researcher, who first drew attention to the activities of the Order Police in the Holocaust.[47] Browning accepts that Jews were treated far worse and were more terribly abused in death camps and in slave labour camps than non-Jewish victims, but he is unwilling to accept a lethal form of anti-Semitism existed within German society which made the Final Solution inevitable once Hitler took power.

A further weakness in Goldhagen's argument is a failure to explain why Hitler's so-called 'willing executioners' were just as willing when asked to kill

Soviet prisoners of war, Gypsies, Poles and many others. Another major problem with Goldhagen's interpretation is his assumption that the German people under the Nazi regime could easily choose not to participate in the killing process without suffering any consequences. It is even difficult to define exactly what Goldhagen means by an 'ordinary' German, especially in the context of the Order Police, which had already been under the control of the SS since the mid-1930s and had undergone a great deal of Nazi indoctrination ever since. Browning has argued that Goldhagen's focus on what he views as 'singular' German cruelty against the Jews actually weakens his case, because if a wider comparative perspective of genocide had been adopted it would have revealed that cruelty and the ability to commit mass murder are not the unique prerogative of 'ordinary Germans'.[48]

Conclusion

In spite of the massive examination of every aspect of Nazi Germany, there remains no single issue which has been completely resolved among historians. In spite of calls by German historians for the Nazi period to be treated like every other period of history, it is still regarded as unique. It is now widely acknowledged that there is unlikely to be any new historical advances through further study of the German archives. Any new insights will be provided only by a broader synthesis of existing writing which integrates political, social and economic factors to produce a new interpretation. The only historian to suggest that Hitler was 'ordinary', perhaps even a 'moderate' among the Nazi Party on many issues, was A. J. P. Taylor, whose views were greeted with howls of protest.

It is possible that the personality of Adolf Hitler and the history of Nazi Germany will eventually lose its massive popular hold over the study of history. In modern-day Germany, there are fewer and fewer people who were actively involved in the Nazi era still alive. Not many years from now, no survivor of the Nazi era will be left. It is unlikely that future generations of Germans will feel obliged to carry the burden for a past they were not responsible for. Outside Germany, all the survivors of Nazi genocide, including all the survivors of the death camps, will also be dead. The day may well arrive when Nazi Germany is just a part of the rest of history. It is to be hoped that when such a day arrives, it will not be accompanied by a cult of hero worship to surround Hitler or the Nazi regime.

It is equally possible that the incredible Nazi phenomenon will never be treated as normal. It may be that each generation will continue to find it abnormal, unique and endlessly fascinating. In a way, the history of Nazi Germany has yet to be written in a detached and objective manner. But in another way, perhaps the history of the Nazi period has already been written. Perhaps the history of Nazi Germany is the most harrowing and emotionally disturbing of all historical subjects: a sort of universal warning and history lesson, which haunts the mind of any person who reads about it. What makes the study of Nazi Germany disturbing is the knowledge that if certain decisions had been taken to stop Hitler coming to power in 1933, and then to stop him building up the arms which brought about the Second World War, then here is one eternal nightmare which could have been prevented.

Notes and references

1 See I. Kershaw, 'Martin Broszat obituary', *German History*, vol. 8, (1990), pp. 310–16.

2 R. Bosworth, *Explaining Auschwitz and Hiroshima. History writing and the Second World War 1945–1990*, London, 1993, p. 83.

3 S. Friedländer, 'Some Germans struggle with memory', in G. H. Hartman (ed.), *Bitburg in moral and political perspective*, Bloomington, MA, 1986, pp. 15–26.

4 For a discussion of the 'historians' debate' see R. J. Evans, *In Hitler's shadow: West German historians and the attempt to escape from the Nazi past*, London, 1989.

5 See H. R. Trevor Roper, 'The mind of Adolf Hitler', Foreword to *Hitler's table talk*, London, 1953.

6 A. Bullock, *Hitler: a study in tyranny*, revised edn, London, 1964.

7 See M. Broszat, *The Hitler state*, London, 1981.

8 I. Kershaw, *Hitler, Vol. 1*, London, 1998.

9 See K. D. Bracher, 'The role of Hitler: perspectives of interpretation', in W. Laqueur (ed.), *Fascism: a reader's guide*, London, 1979, pp. 193–212.

10 Trevor Roper, 'The mind of Adolf Hitler'.

11 See E. Jäckel, *Hitler in history*, London, 1984.

12 A. Hillgruber, *Hitlers Strategie, Politik and Kriegführung 1940–1941*, Frankfurt, 1965.

13 See K. D. Bracher, *The German dictatorship*, London, 1973.

14 H-A. Jacobsen, *Nationalsozialistische Aussenpolitik 1933–1938*, Frankfurt, 1968.

15 Broszat, *Hitler state*.

16 See H. Mommsen, 'National Socialism. Continuity and change', in W. Laqueur (ed.), *Fascism: a reader's guide*, London, 1979, pp. 151–92.

17 A. J. P. Taylor, *The origins of the Second World War*, London, 1961.

18 See F. Fischer, *From Kaiserreich to Third Reich. Elements of continuity in German history 1871–1945*, London, 1986.

19 The debate over continuity is examined in R. Evans, 'From Hitler to Bismarck: Third Reich and Kaiserreich in recent historiography', *Historical Journal*, vol. 26 (1984).

20 See G. Eley, 'Conservatives and Nationalists in Germany: the production of Fascist potentials 1912–1928', in M. Blinkhorn (ed.), *Fascists and conservatives*, London, 1994.

21 Hillgruber, *Hitlers Strategie*.

22 R. Dahrendorf, *Society and democracy in Germany*, London, 1966.

23 D. Schoenbaum, *Hitler's social revolution*, London, 1966.

24 D. Peukert, *Inside Nazi Germany*, London, 1987.

25 See H. Winkler, 'German society, Hitler and the illusion of restoration 1930–1933', *Journal of Contemporary History*, vol. 11 (1976).

26 See I. Kershaw, *The Nazi dictatorship. Problems and perspectives of interpretation*, London, 3rd edn, London, 1993, pp. 147–49.

27 See J. Heyl, 'Hitler's economic thought. A reappraisal', *Central European History*, vol. 6 (1973).

28 K. Hildebrand, *The foreign policy of the Third Reich*, London, 1973; E. Nolte, 'Big business and German politics: a comment', *American Historical Review*, vol. 75 (1969–70), p. 76.

29 See R. Overy, 'Germany, "domestic crisis" and war in 1939', *Past and Present*, vol. 116 (1987), pp. 138–68.

30 See W. Carr, *Arms, autarky and aggression. A study in German foreign policy, 1933–1939*, London, 1979.

31 See A. Schweitzer, *Big business in the Third Reich*, London, 1964.

32 See R. Brady, *The spirit and structure of German Fascism*, London, 1937.

33 Kershaw, *Nazi dictatorship*, pp. 48–49.

34 See T. Mason, 'The primacy of politics – politics and economics in National Socialist Germany', in H. A. Turner (ed.), *Nazism and the Third Reich*, New York, 1972, pp. 175–200.

35 See K. Hildebrand, *The Third Reich*, London, 1979.

36 Overy, 'Germany, "domestic crisis" and war'.

37 See A. Milward, *The German economy at war*, London, 1965.

38 R. J. Overy, 'Hitler's war and the German economy: a reinterpretation', *Economic History Review*, vol. 35 (1982), pp. 272–91.

39 *Ibid.*

40 L. Dawidowicz, *The war against the Jews*, New York, 1975.

41 K. Schleunes, *The twisted road to Auschwitz*, London, 1970.

42 See H. Mommsen, 'The realization of the unthinkable', in G. Hirschfield (ed.), *The politics of genocide*, London, 1986.

43 See D. Irving, *Hitler's war*, London, 1977.

44 M. Broszat, 'Hitler and the genesis of the Final Solution: an assessment of David Irving's thesis', in H. Koch (ed.), *Aspects of the Third Reich*, London, 1985, pp. 390–429.

45 See A. J. Mayer, *Why did the heavens not darken? The Final Solution in history*, New York, 1988.

46 D. Goldhagen, *Hitler's willing executioners. Ordinary Germans and the Holocaust*, London, 1986.

47 See C. R. Browning, *Ordinary men: Reserve Police Battalion 101 and the Final Solution in Poland*, London, 1992.

48 See C. R. Browning, 'Daniel Goldhagen's *Willing Executioners*', *History and Memory*, vol. 30 (1996), pp. 88–109.

Bibliography

The available historical studies of Hitler and Nazi Germany are extremely large. The following list is related to a selection of books and articles on key issues and themes discussed in each chapter of this study.

Original documents

There are a great number of original sources on the history of Nazi Germany. The most extensive collection is: J. Noakes and G. Pridham (eds.), *Nazism 1919–1945. A documentary reader, Vol. 1: The rise to power 1919–1934*, Exeter, 1983; *Vol. 2: State, economy and society*, Exeter, 1984; *Vol. 3: Foreign policy, war and racial extermination*, Exeter, 1988.

Historiographical surveys

There are number of studies which examine the historical debate on Nazi Germany. The most useful are: J. Hiden and J. Farquharson, *Explaining Hitler's Germany. Historians and the Third Reich*, London, 1983; K. Hildebrand, *The Third Reich*, London, 1984; I. Kershaw, *The Nazi dictatorship. Problems and perspectives of interpretation*, 3rd edn, London, 1993.

Adolf Hitler: personality and ideology

There are a vast number of biographies on Adolf Hitler. The most well respected are: A. Bullock, *Hitler. A study of tyranny*, revised edn, London, 1964; W. Carr, *Hitler. A study of personality and politics*, London, 1978; J. Fest, *Hitler*, London, 1974; I. Kershaw, *Hitler*, London, 1998; W. Maser, *Hitler*, London, 1973; N. Stone, *Hitler*, London, 1980; J. Toland, *Adolf Hitler*, New York, 1976. For a detailed examination of Nazi ideology see R. Griffin, *The nature of Fascism*, London, 1990; W. Maser, *Hitler's Mein Kampf*, London, 1970; M. Kitchen, *Fascism*, London, 1976; W. Laquer (ed.), *Fascism: A reader's guide*, London, 1979.

Hitler's rise to power

There are a wide range of studies on the rise to power of Adolf Hitler and the Nazi Party, most notably: W. Allen, *The Nazi seizure of power*, London, 1966; C. Fischer, *The rise of the Nazis*, Manchester, 1995; A. Nicholls, *Weimar and the rise of Hitler*, 2nd edn, London, 1989. A key aspect of Hitler's rise to power concerns Nazi voting support. Useful studies on this subject include: T. Childers, *The Nazi voter*, London, 1983; R. F. Hamilton, *Who voted for Hitler?*, Princeton, 1982. For the role of big business see H. Turner, *Big business and the rise of Hitler*, Oxford, 1985.

The Nazi state

The most useful studies on the nature of power in the Nazi state are: K. D. Bracher, *The German dictatorship*, London, 1973; K. D. Bracher, 'The role of Hitler: perspectives of interpretation', in

W. Laqueur (ed.), *Fascism: A reader's guide*, London, 1979; M. Broszat, *The Hitler state*, London, 1981; I. Kershaw, The *'Hitler myth'. Image and reality in the Third Reich*, London, 1987; H. Mommsen, 'Hitler's position in the Nazi system', in H. Mommsen, *From Weimar to Auschwitz*, Oxford, 1991, pp. 163–68; E. N. Peterson, *The limits of Hitler's power*, Princeton, 1969.

The Nazi economy

There are a number of studies on economic problems in Nazi Germany, including: A. Barkai, *Nazi economics*, London, 1990; A. Millward, *The Nazi economy at war*, London, 1965; R. Overy, *The Nazi economic recovery 1932–1938*, London, 1982; A. Sohn-Rethel, *The economy and class structure of German fascism*, London, 1987; A. Schweitzer, *Big business in the Third Reich*, London, 1964.

Inside Nazi Germany: social and cultural developments

In recent years there have been a number of studies on life inside Nazi Germany, most notably: R. Bessel (ed.), *Daily life in the Third Reich*, Oxford, 1987; D. Peukert, *Inside Nazi Germany*, London, 1987. There are a number of useful social histories of Nazi Germany, including: N. Frei, *Nazi Germany, a social history*, Oxford, 1993; R. Grunberger, *A social history of the Third Reich*, London, 1971; T. Mason, *Social policy in the Third Reich*, London, 1993; D. Shoenbaum, *Hitler's social revolution*, London, 1966. For the role of propaganda see E. Bramstead, *Goebbels and National Socialist propaganda*, London, 1965. For the role of women see C. Koonz, *Mothers in the Fatherland. Women, the family and Nazi politics*, New York, 1976; J. Stephenson, *Women in Nazi society*, London, 1976. For the role of the medical profession see M. Kater, *Doctors under Hitler*, London, 1989. For the role of farmers see J. Farqueharson, *The plough and the swastika*, London, 1976. For the role of the churches see J. Conway, *Nazi persecution of the churches*, London, 1978. For the role of the army see M. Cooper, *The German army, 1933–1945*, London, 1978. For the role of workers see S. Salter, 'Structures of consensus and coercion. Workers' morale and the maintenance of work discipline, 1939–1945', in D. Welch (ed.), *Nazi propaganda. The power and the limitations*, London, 1993.

Foreign policy

There are a vast range of studies on Hitler's foreign policy and its influence on the origins of the Second World War. The standard works remain: W. Carr, *Arms, autarchy and aggression. A study in German foreign policy, 1933–1939*, 2nd edn, London, 1979; K. Hildebrand, *The foreign policy of the Third Reich*, London, 1973; N. Rich, *Hitler's war aims*, 2 vols., London, 1973–74; G. Weinberg, *The foreign policy of Hitler's Germany: Starting World War 2*, London, 1980.

Opposition and resistance

The following books deal with opposition and resistance to the Nazi regime: M. Balfour, *Withstanding Hitler in Germany 1933–1945*, London, 1988; P. Hoffmann, *The German resistance to Hitler*, Cambridge, USA, 1988; D. Large (ed.), *Contending with Hitler. Varieties of German resistance in the Third Reich*, Cambridge, MA, 1991; T. Prittie, *Germans against Hitler*, London, 1964; H. Rothfels, *The German opposition to Hitler*, London, 1961.

Germany at war

There are a number of useful studies of Hitler as war lord, most notably: E. P. Schramm, *Hitler, the man and military leader*, London, 1972; J. Strawson, *Hitler as military commander*, London, 1971. For specific battles and campaigns see J. Keegan, *The Second World War*, London, 1989; E. von Manstein, *Lost victories*, London, 1958. For the crucial German–Russian (Soviet) war see

P. Carell, *Hitler's war on Russia*, 2 vols., London, 1964, 1970; A. Seaton, *The Russo-German war*, London, 1971; F. Ziemke, *Stalingrad to Berlin*, Washington, DC, 1968.

The Holocaust

There are a vast number of studies on the Holocaust, including: P. Baldwin (ed.), *Reworking the past: Hitler, the Holocaust and the historians' debate*, Boston, 1990; Y. Bauer, *The Holocaust in historical perspective*, London, 1978; C. Browning, *The path to genocide. Essays on launching the Final Solution*, Cambridge, 1992; P. Burrin, *Hitler and the Jews. The genesis of the Holocaust*, London, 1993; L. Dawidowicz, *The war against the Jews*, New York, 1975; G. Fleming, *Hitler and the Final Solution*, Oxford, 1986; D. J. Goldhagen, *Hitler's willing executioners. Ordinary Germans and the Holocaust*, London, 1996; R. Hilberg, *The destruction of the Jews* (3 vols.), New York, 1983–85; M. Marrus, *The Holocaust in history*, London, 1988; K. Schleunes, *The twisted road to Auschwitz. Nazi policy towards the Jews*, London, 1965.

Glossary

Abwehr: German military counter-intelligence unit.

Afrika Korps: Special tank unit assembled to help the Italian army in North Africa, led by General Rommel.

Anschluss: Union between Germany and Austria.

Autobahn: Superhighway or motorway.

Blitzkrieg: Lightning war.

Deutsche Arbeiterpartei (DAP): German Workers' Party, founded in 1919 by Anton Drexler; forerunner of the Nazi Party.

Deutsche Arbeitsfront (DAF): The German Labour Front, formed in 1933 as a Nazi replacement for the independent trade unions.

Einsatzgruppen: Task forces. The mobile killing units who carried out massacres of Jews and Communist leaders on the eastern front during the Second World War.

Freikorps: Free Corps. The paramilitary units of ex-soldiers who sprang up all over Germany at the end of the First World War.

Führer: Leader (Adolf Hitler).

Führerbunker: Hitler's underground bunker in Berlin, where the Nazi leader committed suicide in April 1945.

Gauleiter: District leader of the Nazi Party.

Gestapo (*Geheime Staatspolizei*): Secret state police.

Gleichschaltung: Co-ordination. The term used by Nazis to explain the major changes in domestic policy in the early years of the regime.

Hitlerjugend: Hitler Youth.

judenfrei: Jew free. Usually placed on the entrance to towns in Nazi Germany.

Kraft durch Freude: Strength through Joy. The organisation created by the Labour Front to organise recreational activities by workers.

Kristallnacht: Night of Broken Glass. The attack on Jews of 9–10 November 1938.

Lebensraum: Living space. The term used by Hitler to describe his territorial aims.

Luftwaffe: German air-force.

Mittelstand: The middle class.

Nationalsozialistische Deutsche Arbeiterpartei (NSDAP): The National Socialist German Workers' Party, commonly known as the Nazi Party.

Night of the Long Knives: Popular term used to explain the Nazi blood purge of 30 June 1934, when leaders of the SA were murdered.

Ordnungspolizei: Order Police. The uniformed police who played an important role in Nazi genocide killing during the Second World War.

Panzer: The name given to tanks and to tank units.

Reichssicherheitshauptamt (RHSA): Reich Central Security Office.

Reichstag: German parliament.

Reichswehr: The name given to the defensive land army of the Weimar Republic.

Schutzstaffel (SS): Hitler's personal elite bodyguard, dressed in distinctive black uniform, which under the leadership of Heinrich Himmler became the most powerful Nazi organisation within the state.

Sicherheitsdienst (SD): Security branch of the SS, directed by Reinhard Heydrich, which played a crucial role in the organisation of the Holocaust.

Sturmabteilungen (SA): The Nazi storm troopers or 'brown shirts'. The paramilitary private army of the Nazi Party.

Volk: Folk or race.

völkisch: Racial or ethnic.

Völkischer Beobachter: *People's Observer*. The official Nazi daily national newspaper.

Volksgemeinschaft: The folk or people's community. The slogan used by the Nazis to stress a kind of classless national solidarity.

Wehrmacht: German armed forces.

Wehrwirtschaft: War economy.

Weltanschauung: World view, or ideology.

Wolfsschanze: 'The Wolf's Lair'. Hitler's military headquarters in East Prussia.

Zyclon B: The trade name of the cyanide gas crystals used to kill Jews in the extermination camps.

Chronology

1889 *20 April:* Adolf Hitler born in Gasthof zum Pommer, Braunau am Inn, Austria.

1933 *30 January:* Adolf Hitler appointed German Chancellor.

27 February: Reichstag fire.

5 March: Reichstag election results in Nazi victory.

23 March: The 'Enabling Act' passed by the Reichstag, with only the Social Democratic Party voting against it.

1 April: Boycott of Jewish shops (called off a day later after international protest).

10 May: Ceremonial book burning of 'un-German writers', organised by students in Berlin.

June: All political parties, except the NSDAP, are dissolved.

29 July: Hereditary Farm Law.

14 October: Germany withdraws from League of Nations and World Disarmament Conference.

1934 *26 January:* Non-aggression pact with Poland.

30 June: 'Night of the Long Knives'. The blood purge of the SA and other political opponents.

25 July: Dollfuss assassinated in abortive Nazi coup. Hitler denies involvement.

2 August: President Hindenburg dies. Hitler declares himself Führer of the German People. German army swears personal oath of loyalty to Hitler.

1935 *16 March:* Conscription introduced.

11–14 April: Stresa conference: Britain, France and Italy denounce German decision to rearm.

18 June: Anglo-German naval agreement signed.

15 September: Nuremberg Laws deprive Jews of citizenship rights.

1936 *7 March:* German troops occupy demilitarised Rhineland in violation of Locarno Treaty.

1 August: Olympic Games opened by Hitler in Berlin.

9 September: The announcement of the Four Year Plan.

25 October: Rome–Berlin Axis signed.

25 November: Anti-Comintern Pact between Germany and Japan signed (Italy joins on 6 November 1937).

1937 *5 November:* Hitler announces his future war plans to leading service chiefs and foreign minister (Hossbach conference).

19 November: Lord Halifax meets Hitler in order to improve Anglo-German relations.

26 November: Schacht replaced as Economics Minister by Walther Funk.

1938 *4 February:* Blomberg, Minister of War, and Fritsch, army commander-in-chief, both dismissed. Hitler becomes supreme commander of the armed forces.

12 March: German troops march into Austria.

13 March: Anschluss (union with Germany) officially declared.

24 April: Konrad Henlein, leader of the Sudeten German Party, demands 'autonomy' for the Sudeten area of Czechoslovakia.

20 May: The 'May crisis'. Britain, France and the Soviet Union warn Hitler of the consequences of an unprovoked German attack on Czechoslovakia.

30 May: Hitler gives directive to German army for 'the destruction of Czechoslovakia', set for 1 October 1938.

15 September: Chamberlain flies to Germany to meet Hitler at Berchtesgaden to solve the Sudeten crisis.

22 September: Chamberlain meets Hitler at Godesberg. Talks end with no settlement.

29 September: Munich conference: Germany, Britain, Italy and France agree to Sudetenland being incorporated into Nazi Germany.

30 September: Munich agreement signed. Chamberlain declares it is 'peace in our time' on his return to 10 Downing Street.

9 November: Kristallnacht ('Night of Broken Glass'). A night of organised attacks against Jews in Germany.

1939 *20 January:* Schacht dismissed as President of Reichsbank.

30 January: Hitler informs Reichstag that the Jewish 'race in Europe' will be destroyed in the event of a new world war.

15 March: German troops occupy Czechoslovakia.

21 March: Hitler demands return of Danzig from Poland.

31 March: Britain and France offer guarantee to Poland.

22 May: 'Pact of Steel' signed between Germany and Italy.

23 August: Nazi–Soviet pact signed.

1 September: Germany invades Poland.

3 September: Britain and France declare war on Germany.

27 September: Warsaw surrenders.

1940 *9 April:* German occupation of Denmark. Norway invaded by German troops.

10 May: Germany attacks France, Holland, Belgium and Luxembourg.

15 May: Holland surrenders to Germany.

28 May: Belgium surrenders to Germany.

10 June: Italy enters the war. Norway surrenders.

22 June: Franco-German armistice signed.

16 July: Hitler orders 'Operation Sealion' – the invasion of Britain.

15 September: Britain retains air superiority and wins Battle of Britain.

27 September: Tripartite pact signed by Germany, Italy and Japan.

12 October: Hitler calls off 'Operation Sealion'.

28 October: Italy invades Greece.

18 December: Hitler orders army to prepare 'Operation Barbarossa' – the invasion of the Soviet Union.

1941 *2 March:* German troops occupy Bulgaria.

6 April: Germany invades Yugoslavia and Greece.

17 April: Yugoslavia surrenders.

23 April: Greece surrenders.

10 May: Rudolf Hess flies to Scotland on 'peace mission'.

22 June: German invasion of the Soviet Union.

19 September: Jews in Germany required to wear Star of David.

1 December: German army advance is halted before reaching Moscow.

7 December: Japan attacks US fleet at Pearl Harbor.

11 December: Germany and Italy declare war on the USA.

1942 *6 January:* President Roosevelt states the chief US aim of the Second World War is to destroy German militarism.

20 January: Wannsee conference decides on 'Final Solution' of the 'Jewish question'.

21 July: The beginning of the deportation of Jews from the Warsaw ghetto to the extermination camp at Treblinka.

3 November: British victory over Rommel's Afrika Korps at el Alamein.

11 November: German troops occupy Vichy France.

19 November: Major Soviet counteroffensive encircles German army at Stalingrad.

1943 *14 January:* Roosevelt and Churchill demand 'unconditional surrender' of Germany at Casablanca conference.

2 February: German 6th Army surrenders to Red Army at Stalingrad.

19 April: Major uprising by Jews in the Warsaw ghetto (ruthlessly suppressed by German army).

19 May: Berlin declared 'free of Jews'.

24 May: End of German U-boat attacks in Atlantic. Britain and US win Battle of the Atlantic.

5 July: 'Operation Citadel' – German tank battle at Kursk – results in victory for Red Army.

10 July: British and US troops land in Sicily.

25 July: Fall of Mussolini's Fascist rule in Italy.

8 September: Italian government signs armistice with allies.

28 November: Tehran conference of 'Big Three' – Stalin, Roosevelt and Churchill – plans on future of Germany after its 'inevitable' defeat.

1944 *6 June:* D-Day landing – major allied offensive begins with landing at Normandy.

22 June: Major Red Army offensive leads to collapse of German Army Group Centre.

20 July: Bomb attempt by von Stauffenberg on Hitler's life leaves the Nazi leader with only minor injuries.

23 July: The 'Hitler salute' is made compulsory within all ranks of the army.

23 August: The Red Army captures Romania.

8 September: Bulgaria declares war on Germany.

11 September: Anglo-American troops reach the German frontier.

25 September: All able-bodied men in Nazi Germany aged between 16 and 60 called up for the 'People's Militia'.

26 November: Himmler orders destruction of Auschwitz gassing facilities and crematoria.

16 December: Final German offensive of the war begins on the western front in the Ardennes.

1945 *3 January:* US troops begin successful counteroffensive in the Ardennes.

14 January: Red Army offensive reaches East Prussia.

4–11 February: Conference of 'Big Three' at Yalta decides on future division of Germany at the end of the war.

12 February: German women conscripted to serve in the auxiliaries and the 'People's Militia'.

13 February: Massive Anglo-American bomb attack on Dresden.

12 April: President Roosevelt dies suddenly (Harry S. Truman becomes new US President).

25 April: Red Army meets US troops at Torgau on the Elbe river.

30 April: Adolf Hitler commits suicide in his Berlin bunker.

2 May: Grand Admiral Doenitz succeeds Hitler as 'Reich President'.

7 May: Germany signs unconditional surrender to end the Second World War in Europe and the era of Nazi rule in Germany.

Index

DAF (Labour Front), 32, 37
Dahrendorf, Ralf, 127
Dawidowicz, Lucy, 133
death camps, 114–16, 117, 120–1
death penalty, 45; executions of opponents of Nazism, 64, 65, 67–8
death-rates in Nazi Germany, 52, 53
Denmark: Nazi victory over, 88
Dietrich, Marlene, 51
doctors in Nazi Germany, 52
Dollfuss, Engelbert, 71
Drexler, Anton, 10

eastern Europe: and Hitler's foreign policy, 71, 75, 79, 80, 126, 131; Hitler's plans for *Lebensraum* in, 15, 125; *see also* Czechoslovakia; Poland
Ebert, Friedrich, 16
Eckart, Dietrich, 10
economic crisis: in the Weimar Republic, 17, 21
economy in Nazi Germany, 32–9, 41; and businesses, 35–6; and farmers, 36–7; Four Year Plan (1936), 34–5, 129, 131; historical debate on the, 129–31; and industrial workers, 37–8; and living standards, 38–9, 41–2; 'New Plan', 33–4; policies, 32–3; unemployment and inflation, 34; war economy (*Wehrwirtschaft*), 33, 35
'Edelweiss Pirates' (*Edelweisspiraten*), 65
education in Nazi Germany, 46–7, 55
Eichmann, Adolf, 113
Eisenhower, Dwight D., 98, 100
Eisner, Kurt, 9
Eley, Geoffrey, 126–7
elites in Germany: and the Nazi 'social revolution', 127, 128
employment of women in Nazi Germany, 48–9
Enabling Act (1933), 26, 63
euthanasia programme (1939–41), 109–10

families in Nazi Germany, 45–6
farmers: and Nazi economic policy, 34, 36–7
Feder, Gottfried, 10, 11
films in Nazi Germany, 50–1
Final Solution, *see* Holocaust (Final Solution)
First World War (1914–18), 8–9, 51, 107
Fischer, Fritz, 126
folk community ideology, 13–14, 18, 127
food expenditure in Nazi Germany, 38–9
Foreign Office: opponents of Nazi regime at the, 59
foreign policy, 70–85; bilateral diplomacy, 71; German, 126–7; historical debate on, 125–7; Hitler's aims, 14–15, 71; and the Munich agreement (1938), 59, 78–80; and the occupation of the Rhineland, 73, 75, 82–3
Four Year Plan (1936), 34–5, 129, 131

France: and the Czech crisis, 77, 78, 79, 80; and Hitler's foreign policy, 15, 71, 72, 73; and Hitler's invasion of Poland, 87; Hitler's views on, 82; and the Second World War, 82, 87–9; and the Spanish Civil War, 74
Franco, General Francisco, 74
Frank, Hans, 117, 132
Frederick the Great, king of Prussia, 4
Frick, Wilhelm, 24, 132
Friedländer, Saul, 123
Fritsch, Colonel-General von, 76–7

gangs: street gangs in Nazi Germany, 65
Gauleiter (local governors), 31
genocide: and the Holocaust, 131–2
German army: and conscription, 72; and the conspiracy to kill Hitler, 60–1; and Hitler in Bavaria, 10; Hitler and the First World War, 8–9; Hitler takes charge of the, 76–7; and Hitler as war lord, 86–7; and the Nazi Party, 11, 44; and Nazi radicals, 26–7, 128; and the Nazi 'social revolution', 128; and the Night of the Long Knives, 27; occupation of the Rhineland, 73, 75, 82–3; and the power structure of the Nazi economy, 130; rearmament programme, 33–4, 35, 41–2, 70, 72; resistance in the, 58–9
German Girls' League, 48
German National People's Party, 25–6
German nationalism: Hitler's adoption of, 3–4, 7, 8; and Hitler's ideology, 13–14, 15, 19; and the Nazi Party programme, 11
German people: responsibility for the Holocaust, 113–14, 135–6
German Women's Enterprise, 49
Gestapo, 27, 44–5, 110, 133; and resistance to Nazism, 62, 63, 64, 67–8
Giesler, Paul, 64
Goebbels, Joseph, 20, 30, 49; and the Anschluss, 77; jokes about, 65; and *Kristallnacht*, 109; on the Nazi regime and the press, 53–4; and propaganda, 49–50, 53; suicide of, 49, 100–1; views on women, 48
Goerdeler, Dr Carl Friedrich, 58, 59
Goldhagen, Daniel, 135–6
Göring, Hermann, 11, 24, 25, 30, 70, 76, 132; and the Four Year Plan, 34; and the Night of the Long Knives, 27
graffiti in Nazi Germany, 65

Halder, General Franz, 86, 94
Halifax, Lord, 75–6
Hanisch, Reinhold, 6–7
Hansen, Colonel Georg, 60
Hassell, Ulrich von, 59
health: of Hitler, 29–30; in Nazi Germany, 52–3
Herbert, A. P., 91–2
Hereditary Farm Law (1933), 36–7

Index

Index

Scholl, Sophie, 63, 64
schools in Nazi Germany, 46–7, 55
Schuschnigg, Kurt von, 77
Schweitzer, A., 129
SD (*Sicherheitsdienst*), 44, 45, 110, 133
Second World War, 44, 86–105; Ardennes
  offensive (1944–45), 99; in the Balkans, 91;
  Battle of Britain (1940), 89–90; and the
  Catholic church, 58; D-Day, 98–9; defeat of
  Nazi Germany, 99–100; defeat of Poland, 87;
  fall of Denmark and Norway, 87–8;
  historical debate on causes of, 125–6, 130–1;
  and Hitler as war lord, 86–7; and the July
  plot (1944), 60–1, 68; military defeats for
  Axis powers (1942–44), 97–8; and the Nazi
  economy, 130–1; Nazi victory in western
  Europe (1940), 88–9; in North Africa, 91;
  outbreak of, 81–2; phases of, 86; Phoney
  War, 87; and the Soviet Union, 90, 91, 92–4,
  97–8; war economy (*Wehrwirtschaft*), 33, 35;
  and women in Nazi Germany, 48–9
Seyss-Inquart, Arthur, 77
Shaw, George Bernard, 51
slave labour in Nazi Germany, 114, 116, 130
small businesses: and Nazi economic policy,
  36
Social Democratic Party: and the 1933
  election, 24, 25; in Austria, 7; and the
  Enabling Act, 26; and the Nuremberg Laws,
  118; resistance to Nazism, 63, 66; in the
  Weimar Republic, 16, 18
social revolution: debate on Nazi Germany as
  a, 127–9
socialism: and Hitler's ideology, 14, 21; and
  the Nazi Party, 11
SOPADE reports, 63
Soviet prisoners of war, Nazi treatment of, 117,
  134
Soviet Union: and the battle of Stalingrad, 96,
  103; and the Czech crisis, 77, 78, 79; and the
  Final Solution, 134; and Hitler as war lord,
  86, 87; and Hitler's foreign policy aims, 72,
  75, 126; and Hitler's ideas on 'Jewish
  Bolshevism', 14, 134; Hitler's invasion of the
  (Operation Barbarossa), 90, 91, 92–4, 102;
  mass shootings of Jews in the, 112–13; Nazi
  offensive against (Operation Citadel), 97–8;
  and the Nazi–Soviet pact, 81, 84, 87, 90; and
  negotiations for an Anglo-Soviet alliance,
  81; Red Army offensive against the Nazis,
  98–9; and the Spanish Civil War, 74
Spanish Civil War, 73–5
SS (*Schutzstaffel*), 26, 27, 44, 45; and the army,
  44; *Einsatzgruppen*, 112–13, 119; and the Final
  Solution, 133, 134, 136; and the Nazi 'social
  revolution', 128; and the persecution of the
  Jews, 110, 111, 112
Stalin, Joseph, 79, 90, 97, 99; and the
  Nazi–Soviet pact, 81, 84

Stalingrad, battle of (1942–43), 96, 103
Stauffenberg, Colonel Claus Graf Schenk von,
  60, 61, 68
sterilisation, compulsory, 46
Strasser, Gregor, 17, 20, 21, 27, 37, 128
Strauss, Richard, 51
Stresa Front (1935), 72, 73
Stresemann, Gustav, 70
structuralist/functionalist historians, 124–5;
  on Hitler's foreign policy, 125–6
'Swing Youth', 65

Taylor, A. J. P., 126, 136
teachers, 47
Thälmann, Ernst, 19
theatre in Nazi Germany, 51
Tresckow, Henning von, 60, 61
Trevor Roper, Hugh (Lord Dacre), 124, 125
Trott zu Solz, Adam von, 59, 62

unemployment: and Nazi economic policies,
  33, 34; and Nazi Party support, 19; in the
  Weimar Republic, 17, 21
United States: and Hitler's foreign policy aims,
  125
universities, 47, 53; students and the White
  Rose Movement, 63–4

Versailles Treaty (1919), 9; and German
  foreign policy (1918–33), 70; and Hitler's
  foreign policy aims, 14–15, 72, 125; and the
  Nazi Party programme, 11
Vienna: Hitler in, 5–8
Vienna Academy of Fine Arts, 5, 6
Volkswagen cars, 38

wages in Nazi Germany, 37
Wagner, Richard, 5, 51
Wannsee conference (1942), 113
Wehler, Hans-Ulrich, 126
Weimar Republic: and Bavaria, 9–10; and
  economic crisis, 17, 21; foreign policy of the,
  70; and Hitler, 9; and the Jews, 107;
  vulnerability of the democratic system of
  the, 15–17
White Rose Movement, 63–4, 67
Winkler, H., 128–9
Winter Relief, 43
Witzleben, Field Marshal Erwin von, 60
women in Nazi Germany, 46, 48–9, 55–6
working class: and Nazi electoral support,
  18–19; and the Nazi 'social revolution', 128
working conditions in Nazi Germany, 37–8

young people, 32, 47–8, 54, 65; anti-Nazi
  youth groups, 64–5

Zeitzler, General Kurt, 96
Zhukov, General Georgi, 94, 96, 97–8, 100